P9-DBZ-172

# RUSSIA WILL
# ATTACK ISRAEL
## - Ray Comfort

Copyright February 1991
Ray Comfort
For The Thinking Mind Publications
P.O. Box 1172
Bellflower, CA 90706

Printed in the United States of America
ISBN 1-878859-05-6
Cover design -- Steve Hunt
Illustrations -- Paul Clarkson

This book is dedicated to Bob Elliff, Beckie Conn, Robert & Trish Trivison and family, my Aunt Bea, and to my lovely wife Sue.

## CHAPTERS

# Chapter 1
# THE WISDOM OF SKEPT-ICISM

At the beginning of each year, predictably, the news media parade a long line of those who profess to know the future. With hit and miss prophecies, the procession moves from palm-reading, ball-gazing gypsies to respectably-dressed, clean-cut astrologers, in an effort to bring some clue to what the immediate hereafter holds for humanity. In the thick fog of the future, now and then someone says something that actually comes to pass. Take for instance the 16th century prophet, Nostradamus. He predicted the future with an uncanny accuracy -- "Pasteur will be celebrated as a godlike figure. This is when the moon completes her great cycle." In 1889 Louis Pasteur made a vital contribution to medical science. The lunar cycle takes 19 years to go around the earth. One such cycle was completed in 1889. He predicted the great fire of London nearly a century after his death -- "The blood of the just will be demanded of London. Burnt by fire in three times twenty plus six." The disaster happened in 1666. Nostradamus adopted the Italian habit of leaving out the first two digits of the date. He predicted the rise of Napoleon, Louis XIV, Charles 1st, the plague of London and the bombing of Hiroshima . . . all with incredible detail.

Nostradamus also predicted several extraordinarily accurate details about Adolf Hitler. One sums up Hitler's life and even predicts the fact that his death, in Berlin in 1945, would never be satisfactorily confirmed -- "In the mountains of Austria near the Rhine, there will be born of simple parents a man who will claim to defend Poland and Hungary, and whose fate will never be certain. Beast wild and hungry will cross the rivers; the great part of the battlefield will be against Hister." He blew it somewhat by describing Hitler as "Hister," saying he was the second antichrist, Napoleon being the first, with one more antichrist to rise. He also states that there will be a Third World

War, which will be fought in the Northern Hemisphere, climaxing with the words, "From the sky will come the Great King of Terror!" He even gives the date.

There are prophets of old who predicted (when Russia was just a tribal people), that they would swoop down upon Israel and seek to destroy it as a nation. The credibility of these prophets was not judged upon how often they were right, but how often they were wrong. The qualification in those days was a life and death issue. If the prophecy didn't come to pass, the "prophet" was to be put to death.

These seers clearly predicted that Russia would attack Israel, but before we look at the details of what they said, I want to prove to you that their writings are different from all others within the annals of information. Personally, I'm a skeptic, and I hope you are also. Too many of the masses are wide-eyed and naive, and have been led down the path of gullible's travels. I want to know if something is totally trustworthy before I will put my faith in it. So I'm going to give you information to weigh within your mind. How can you know whether these writings are trustworthy; is there any way of finding out if they are supernaturally inspired -- were they written by man or by God?

When a man writes a letter, does *he* write it or does his pen? Obviously, he writes the letter, and the pen is the instrument he uses. The claim of these men, is that it was *God* who did the writing, while they were the instruments He used. If these 66 books (collectively called the Bible), written by 40 men, are indeed the word of our Creator, and they claim that immortality is a free gift, then we would be fools not to at least give them a fleeting glance. But if they are merely an historical account, the writings of men, they need to be exposed as fraudulent; as millions have been deceived by them.

The irony of the Christian faith is that it *seems* to be intellectual suicide, but proves to be the ultimate intellectual challenge. What we will do to begin with, is look at four sets of amazing facts:

1/ Scientific,
2/ General,
3/ Prophetic,
4/ Politically prophetic.

Before we do, realize that the Bible was written by these 40 men, over a period of 1600 years, beginning at 1500 B.C. Its continual claim is that these men were inspired by God (2 Peter 1:21 -- *reference to The Holy Bible, King James Version*).

If this is correct, this should be no ordinary book. In the light of these thoughts, let's look at the following:

## SCIENTIFIC FACTS:

1/ At a time when science taught that the earth sat on a large animal or a giant (1500 B.C.), the Bible spoke of the earth's free float in space, "He . . . hangeth the earth upon nothing" (Job 26:7).

2/ When twentieth-century man has just begun to understand the existence of the ozone layer (an invisible shield that protects the earth from the harmful rays of the sun), the Bible mentioned it in 800 B.C. "The shields of the earth belong unto the Lord" (Psalm 47:9).

3/ The prophet Isaiah also tells us (Isaiah 40:22) that the earth is round -- "It is He who sitteth upon the circle of the earth." Secular man discovered this 2400 years later.

4/ Not too many people realize that radio waves and light waves are two different forms of the same thing. God told this fact to Job in the year 1500 B.C., "Canst thou send lightnings, that they may go and say unto thee, Here we are?" Who would have

believed that light could be sent and actually speak? This was first realized in 1864 when "the British scientist James Clerk Maxwell suggested that electricity and light waves were two forms of the same thing" (*Modern Century Illustrated Encyclopedia* Vol. 12).

5/ The Book of Job is very specific in its description of light saying, "Where is the way where light dwells" (Job 38:19). Modern man has only just discovered that light has a "way," involving motion traveling at 186,000 miles per second.

**6/** Science has now discovered that stars send out radio waves. These are received on earth as a high pitch. God mentioned this in Job 38:7 " . . . when the morning stars sang together . . . "

**7/** When science is in the dark as to why the dinosaur disappeared, the Bible would seem to shed

light on the subject. In Job 40:15-24, God Himself speaks, describing the largest of all the creatures He made. He speaks of this massive animal as being herbivorous (plant-eating), having its strength in its hips, a tail like a large tree, very strong bones, a habitat among trees, able to consume large amounts of water, and being of great height.

Then the Scriptures say, " . . . He who made him can make his sword to approach unto him." In other words, God brought extinction to this huge prehistoric creature.

8/ "Most cosmologists (scientists who study the structure and evolution of the universe) agree that the Genesis account of creation, in imagining an initial void, may be uncannily close to the truth." (*Time,* Dec. 1976).

9/ We are told that science expresses the universe in five terms: time, space, matter, power and motion. The Book of Genesis Chapter 1 revealed such truths to the Hebrews in 1450 B.C. "In the beginning (time) God created the Heaven (space) and the earth (matter) . . . And the Spirit (power) of God moved (motion) upon the face of the waters." In the next chapter, we will look at further evidence to substantiate the fact that the Bible is more than just a history book.

# Chapter 2
# TEN THOUSAND DOLLARS

In Chapter 1 we looked at some of the remarkable scientific facts in the Scriptures. Now we will continue by looking at more general elements:

1/ In Genesis Chapter 6, God gave Noah the dimensions of the one million, three hundred thousand cubic square foot ark he was to build. In 1609 at Hoorn in Holland, a ship was built after that same pattern, and this revolutionized shipbuilding. By the year 1900 every large ship on the high seas was definitely inclined towards the proportions of the ark (as verified by "Lloyd's Register of Shipping" in the *World Almanac)*.

2/ God asked Job a strange question in Job 38:22, "Hast thou entered into the treasures of the snow?" This didn't make too much sense to us until the advent of the microscope, revealing the incredible beauty of snow crystals.

3/ Two prophecies (Genesis 49:1,20 &

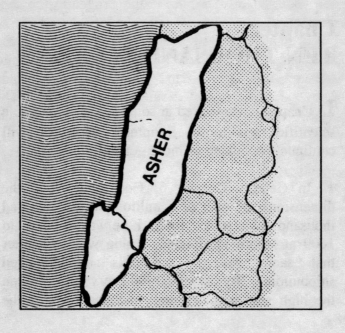

Deuteronomy 33:24), written around 3,000 years B.C., combine to tell us, "In the latter days . . . Asher . . . let him dip his foot in oil." As one studies a map of the tribe of Asher, it perfectly resembles a foot poised to dip. In 1935 the Great International Iraq Petroleum Enterprise opened precisely at the base of the foot, pumping a million gallons of oil a day to the Haifa harbor.

4/ In the Book of Beginnings, in Genesis Chapter 16, God said that Ishmael (the progenitor of the Arab race, see *Time*, April 4, 1988) would be a "wild man, and every man's hand will be against him; and he shall dwell in the presence of all his brethren." Four thousand years later, who could deny that this prophecy is being fulfilled in the Arab race? The Arabs and the Jews are "brethren" having the same ancestors. The whole cause of Middle East conflict is because they are dwelling together.

5/ In Isaiah 66:7-8 (700 B.C.), the Prophet gives a strange prophecy, "Before she travailed, she brought forth; before her pain came, she was delivered of a man-child; who hath heard such a thing? Who hath seen such things? Shall the earth be made to bring forth in one day? Or shall a nation be born at once? For as soon as Zion travailed, she brought forth her children." In 1922 the League of Nations gave Great Britain the mandate (political authority) over Palestine. On May 14, 1948, Britain withdrew her mandate, and the nation of Israel was "born in a day." There are more than 25 Bible prophecies concerning Palestine that have been literally fulfilled. Probability computer estimations conclude that the chances of these being accidentally fulfilled are more than one chance in 33 million.

6/ In 1905, Scotland Yard in England launched into a new era of scientific detection. At a murder trial, Detective Inspector Stockley Collins explained to the jury that skin patterns could provide up to 20 characteristics on a single finger. Over 10 years, he had examined a million fingerprints and never found more than three identical characteristics on the fingers of any two people. They discovered that every single man has a seal, an imprint on his hand, which can show other men crimes he has committed. The Book of Job tells us this amazing fact many thousands of years before Scotland Yard discovered it:

-- "He (God) sealeth up the hand of every man, that all men may know his work" (Job 37:7).

**7/** In spring of 1947, the *Dead Sea Scrolls* were discovered. These manuscripts were copies of large portions of the Old Testament, a thousand years older than any other existing copies. Study of the scrolls has revealed that the Bible hasn't changed in content down through the ages as many skeptics had surmised.

Many times I have heard the statement that the Bible is "full of mistakes." Over the years I have spent literally thousands of hours searching the Scriptures, and I can't find them. In fact, if you can prove to me that there is even one mistake in the Word of God, I will give you $10,000 cash.

## PROPHETIC FACTS

As I have said, Bible Law states that if a prophet was not 100% accurate in his prophecy, he was to be put to death. Nostradamus would have been stoned to death as a false prophet. If the Bible is the Book of the Creator, its prophecies will be perfectly accurate. Now bear in mind the faultless description the Bible gives of this day and age in which we live (the "latter days"), as we look at the "signs of the times."

These signs are to warn us of the coming Day when Almighty God reveals Himself to humanity; when His everlasting Kingdom comes to earth, and

His will is done on earth, "as it is in Heaven."

1/ False Bible teachers will be money hungry, be
smooth talkers, have many followers, and will slur
the Christian faith (2 Peter 2:1-3). Want a dose of
nausea? Tune into "Christian," television and learn
how to prosper. The whole key is in giving. The
trouble is, *you* are the one who does the giving. The
ministries would cut a little more credibility if they
were the ones who did the giving. Wouldn't it be
refreshing to hear a T.V. evangelist say, "I believe
in 'seed faith.' In fact, I believe so much in the
principle, this week *we* are going to be doing the
planting. You can see the number on the screen,
call in and we will plant money in the soil of your
bank account." Hen's teeth. When I have heard
the phrase, "Give generously . . . or I won't be
here next week," my earnest prayer has been,"Yes
Lord. . . *please,* don't let him be here next week."
My prayers are slowly being answered.

Still there are some who hang on. *USA TODAY*
printed the following article: "Move over Jimmy
Swaggart . . . Robert Tilton is now the USA's
fastest-growing force in T.V. evangelism. Five days
a week, this 44-year-old former drug abuser turned
preacher appears on 91 T.V. stations nationwide to
plug his prosperity gospel -- coaxing viewers to

"vow $1,000 unto the Lord" and be blessed. He pierces airwaves with prayers so ferocious his body quakes, face contorts, neck veins strain. His words shift from English to "tongues." His preaching style and claims of cures and wealth surpass anything else now seen on evangelistic T.V. In return for a "$1,000 vow," he says, his prayers cast out demons, cure disease and yield cash and shiny new cars for the truly faithful.

"But Jeffery Hadden, University of Virginia televangelism expert, says, Tilton has "gone well beyond the prosperity gospel . . . and crossed over the line into sham." Offering an opinion echoed privately by other televangelists, Hadden says: "If there's an analogy to the trash of T.V. talk, this is religious trash. It's the most incredible upfront show game I have ever seen." Tilton has a $5.25 million home. He and his wife have their own Mercedes.

2/ Homosexuality will be increasingly evident at the end of the age (2 Timothy 3:3). At present there are reported to be 17,000,000 homosexuals in the U.S.

3/ Earthquakes will increase (Matthew 24:7). Science estimates that there are a million earthquakes each year, with up to twenty going on simultaneously at any moment. Between 1940 and 1950 there were four "killer" earthquakes. Between 1950 and 1960 there were nine. From the years 1960 to 1970 there were thirteen. Between 1970 and 1980 there were fifty-six; and between 1980 and 1990 there were seventy four.

4/ There will be an increase in heart attacks, resulting in death (Luke 21:26). Who could deny that fact? Almost every night on television, advertisements remind us about our intake of cholesterol and fats, and give statistics so frightening it could cause heart-failure.

5/ Many wars will erupt (Matthew 24:6). There have been over 100 wars since 1945, with over 16 million deaths. In actuality, there are so many wars going on at any given moment around the world, they don't even merit mention on the news.

6/ The Bible warns that these times will reveal much increase in the occult (1 Timothy 4:1). In the United States there is enough business to keep 10,000 astrologers working full-time, and an additional 175,000 astrologers working part-time.

Halloween is as popular as Christmas. Horoscopes are in almost every newspaper, and on

television. Many top-selling books, movies and rock groups extol satanism and other occultic activities.

**7/** People will forsake the Ten Commandments as a moral code, committing adultery, stealing, lying, and killing (Matthew 24:12). *USA TODAY* reported that a survey revealed just over 50% of men have committed adultery, with women not too far behind. U.S. law in most states still allows the taking of the lives of unborn children. In 1980, the high-school graduates numbered 3 million, yet in 1991 they had dropped by 600,000. This co-relates with the Roe-vs-Wade legislation which legalized abortion in the mid-seventies; a decade which yielded the lowest birth-rate this century. In other words, because U.S. civil law ignored the Divine Law, "You shall not kill," 600,000 Americans are not around to graduate.

In Pittsburgh, a young man, just 18 years old decided that he and his friends could make some extra cash by robbing an elderly couple for whom he had done some odd jobs. The gang tied the couple to chairs, then ransacked the home.

The 18 year old didn't want the victims to identify them to the police, so he decided to kill them. First, he arranged the chairs to face each other, then he cut the woman's throat. As the husband cried out and wept, the youth did the same to the old man. He then left them there in their chairs to watch each other bleed to death.

The Pittsburgh murders were not isolated cases of violence. Horrific murders have become commonplace and are a biblical sign of the end of this age. Recently there were 2300 murders in one year in the city of Los Angeles.

8/ There will be a cold, religious system, denying

God's power (2 Timothy 3:5). The Bible puts it this way, " . . . having a form of godliness, but denying the power thereof." In other words they will have some sort of faith in God, but they will deny the supernatural aspect both of God and of His Word. Many of the traditional churches have, especially in countries like the U.K. and Europe, become nothing more than museums, existing for the pleasure of stained-glass-gazing tourists.

9/ Other first century prophets proclaim that men will substitute fantasy in place of Christian truth (2 Timothy 4:4). This is so evident at Christmas when the birth of the Savior is lost behind the myth of Santa Claus.

10/ Deadly diseases will be prevalent (Matthew 24:7). The former U.S. Surgeon-General C. Everett Koop confirmed estimations that 100,000,000 will die of Aids by 1997. 160,000 Americans die of cancer each year.

11/ The fact that God once flooded the earth (the Noahic flood) will be denied (2 Peter 3:5).

12/ The institution of marriage will be forsaken (1 Tim. 4:3).

**13/** There will be an increase in famines (Matt. 14:7). It is estimated that 40,000 children die every day through malnutrition, much of it caused by political policies rather than for a lack of food.

**14/** Interest in vegetarianism will increase (1 Tim.4:3).

**15/** There will be a cry for peace (1 Thessalonians 5:3).

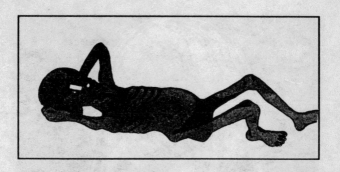

**16/** Knowledge (Hebrew, "science") will greatly increase (Daniel 12:4).

**17/** There will be hypocrites in the Church (Matthew 13:25-30).

**18/** Stress will be part of living in the "latter days" (2 Timothy 3:1).

**19/** There will be increase in religious cults (Matthew 24:11). Cults are growing at an incredible rate in the United States. To date, over 2,000 groups now claim up to 10 million members, thanks to deceptive recruiting techniques, says a prominent psychologist. Margaret T. Singer of the University of California at Berkley, who has counselled more than 700 cult members, says many cults are becoming wealthy and, consequently, much more

powerful than ever. She says cults are moving into the suburbs, especially at private schools, where unsuspecting students are more susceptible.

Hare Krishnas are wearing wigs at airports where they collect donations, sometimes saying they are working for the YMCA. The Church Of Scientology hangs posters asking parents, "Would you like your child to read better?" in an effort to lure children into the program with their parents' unknowing blessing. The Unification Church, headed by Rev. Sun Yung Moon, has a vast empire of convenience stores, real estate, newspapers and other businesses that make over $200 million each year, partly by hiring young people, converting them to their religion and paying them a fraction of the minimum wage.

The Mormon Church has grown from 30 members in 1830 to more than 4,000,000 as of April, 1978. Their projected growth rate for the year 2,000 is 8,000,000. They will get it too; with their massive television campaign, using advertisements that fade out the Bible and fade in the *Book of Mormon.* Their aim is to make the cult seem "Christian." And they do seem very Christian to those who don't know that they believe God has a wife, that Jesus is the brother of Satan, that they deny the virgin birth, that God came down and had sex with Mary, and a hundred and one other strange concepts that defy the imagination.

The Jehovah's Witnesses are also growing at a startling rate. The group was started in 1879 by Charles Russel, who claimed that he had Jehovah's divine guidance to re-establish His church on earth. They now have a world-wide membership of 3 million, and like most cults, claim they are the only ones on earth who have the truth.

One of their means of obtaining converts, is to

point to the fulfillment of Bible prophecy.

What they don't tell you, is that if you do adhere to their doctrine, you won't be allowed to associate with any ex-Jehovah's Witnesses. Neither will you be allowed to vote, salute the flag, sing the national anthem, serve in the military in any way, celebrate Christmas, Mother's day, birthdays etc., give blood to your dying child, think for yourself on Biblical issues, or question *Watchtower* teachings.

Neither do they tell you that they have their own version of the Bible, in which they have changed major portions of scripture, particularly regarding the deity of Jesus Christ.

20/ There will be much intimidation from nation to nation (Matthew 24:7).

21/ The future will seem fearful to many (Luke 21:26). In January of 1991, the media reported the tragic death of a woman who was so fearful of the future, she loaded her three sons and her 3-year-old daughter into the family's minivan and drove to the secluded San Pedro point at the waterfront of the Los Angeles Harbor. She stopped the van at the red curb that faces the water and let the engine idle for a moment. Then she backed up 300 feet, turned on her high beams and put the accelerator to the floor.

"There was a little screech of the tires, like burning rubber, and then whooooooooom," said Tom Kenourgios, a film location coordinator who was drinking coffee and reading a newspaper when he saw the van rocket into the harbor at something like 60 m.p.h.

The reason the 34 year old took her life and the lives of her children was solely because she feared the future, not only for herself, but for her children. For many, the future is hopeless.

22/ Humanity will become materialistic (2 Tim.3:5).

23/ There will be many involved in travel (Daniel 12:4). In the year of 1988, citizens of the U.S. spent approximately $32.9 billion on international travel.

24/ The Christian Gospel will be preached as a warning to all nations (Matthew 24:14).

25/ Christians will be hated (Luke 21:17).

26/ Many who profess to be Christians will fall away from their faith (Matthew 24:10).

27/ There will be "signs in the sun" (Luke 21:25).

This is possibly a reference to an increase in sun spots which, according to the dictionary, are "dark, irregular spots appearing periodically on the sun's surface."

**28/** There will be an increase in pestilence. There is so much pestilence in and on the soil, it is commonplace to spray poisons on our fruit trees and food crops. In fact in the U.S. 390,000 tons of pesticides are sprayed on crops each year *(U.S. News*, Nov. 16, '87).

**29/** Youth will become rebellious (2 Timothy 3:2). During the late fifties and early sixties, youth exploded into new realms of rebellion, drugs and what was commonly called the "sexual revolution." The revolution wasn't just against Judeo-Christian morality, but against all forms of authority.

**30/** Men will mock the signs of the end of the age with this philosophy, "These signs have always been around." This will be because they fail to understand that God is not subject to the dimension of time (2 Peter 3:4).

The sign which is the culmination of all these signs will be the Israeli occupation of Jerusalem

(Luke 21:14). In 1869, when the Suez Canal opened, the United Kingdom gained better seaborne access to its important possession of India, whose borders were becoming increasingly threatened by the southward expansion of imperial Russia. Britain, by intervention in Egypt and by treaty with the small Sheikhdoms of the Arabian Peninsula, made a number of alliances to guarantee the safety of its sea routes. With the collapse of the Ottoman Empire following the end of World War I, the occupying

European powers carved up the area under a mandate system established by the League of Nations. In 1920 it authorized Great Britain to set up a postwar government in Iraq. Britain drew the new country's boundaries according to its strategic needs, mostly around old Ottoman provinces. The foreign presence rallied the Iraqis and awakened a sense of national pride that would eventually drive the British from Iraq.

Kuwait, which was governed by the Sabah dynasty (founded in the 18th century), had also been part of the Ottoman Empire. Under British protection since 1899, Kuwait gained complete independence in 1961.

After the end of World War 2 thousands of Jews began to pour into Palestine. Zionists had pushed for the creation of a Jewish homeland there for many years. However, Palestinian Arabs resented the new settlers, and there began a friction which eventually caused the United Nations to propose dividing the British mandate of Palestine into separate Arab and Jewish states. Arabs strongly opposed the plan, but in 1948 when Great Britain withdrew because of high costs in policing that state among other things, Israel declared itself a state.

It was big news. *The New York Times* carried the headline "ZIONISTS PROCLAIM NEW STATE

OF ISRAEL . . . The Jews Rejoice." Then on Thursday, June 8th, 1967, the newspaper announced, "ISRAELIS ROUT THE ARABS APPROACH SUEZ, BREAK BLOCKADE, OCCUPY OLD JERUSALEM . . . Israelis Weep and Pray Beside the Wailing Wall. Israeli troops wept and prayed today at the foot of the Wailing Wall -- the last remnant of Solomon's Second Temple and the object of pilgrimage by Jews through the centuries.

"In battle dress and still carrying their weapons, they gathered at the base of the sand-colored wall and sang Haltel, a series of prayers reserved for occasions of great joy.

"They were repeating a tradition that goes back 2,000 years but has been denied Israeli Jews since 1948, when the first of three wars with the Arabs ended in this area.

"The wall is all that remains of the Second temple, built in the 10th century before Christ and destroyed by the Romans in A.D. 70.

"The Israelis, trembling with emotion, bowed vigorously from the waist as they chanted psalms in a lusty chorus. Most had submachine guns slung over their shoulders and several held bazookas as they prayed.

"Among the leaders to pray at the wall was Maj.

Gen. Moshe Dayan, the new Defence Minister. He told reporters, "We have returned to the holiest of our holy places, never to depart from it again."

To many it was of little real significance, but to Bible scholars around the world it was of tremendous importance. The Jewish people, after over 1900 years without a homeland, occupied Israel. In 1967 they set foot in Jerusalem fulfilling the words of Jesus Christ spoken 2,000 years earlier.

God warned that if the Jews forsook His Law, He would scatter them throughout the earth, allowing them to be put to shame, then draw them back to Israel (Ezekiel 36:24). The Bible makes special reference to the Jews being drawn back to Israel from "the north country" (Jeremiah 23:7-8). The nation of Israel is the night-light on the clock of Bible prophecy. It shows us how close we are to the "midnight hour." David Ben-Gurion, the first prime minister and minister of defence in Israel, made this statement: "Ezekiel 37 has been fulfilled, and the nation Israel is hearing the footsteps of the Messiah."

# Chapter 3
# RUSSIA AND ISRAEL

A number of books of the Bible speak of future events. Ezekiel Chapter 38 (written approx. 600 B.C.) prophecies that in these times, i.e. the "latter days" the "prince of Meshech," would combine with Iran, Libya (in Hebrew called "Put"), and Communistic Ethiopia (in Hebrew called "Cush") and attack Israel. According to this portion of scripture, this will take place after an Israeli peace initiative has been successful. For your own interest, I will quote the relevant verses of this chapter:

*"And the word of the Lord came unto me, saying, Son of man, set thy face against Gog, the land of*

37

*Magog, the chief prince of Meshech and Tubal, and prophecy against him, and say, Thus saith the Lord GOD; Behold, I am against thee, O Gog, the chief prince of Meshech and Tubal: And I will turn thee back, and put hooks into thy jaws, and I will bring thee forth, and all thine army, horses and horsemen, all of them clothed with all sorts of armour, even a great company with bucklers and shields, all of them handling swords: Persia, Ethiopia, and Libya with them; all of them with shield and helmet: Gomer*

*with all his bands; the house of Togarmah of the north quarters, and all his bands: and many people with thee . . . After many days thou shalt be visited: the latter years thou shalt come into the land that is brought back from the sword, and is gathered out of many people, against the mountains of Israel, which have been always waste: but it is brought forth out of the nations, and they shall dwell safely all of them . . . Thou shalt ascend and come like a storm, thou shalt be like a cloud to cover the land, thou, and all thy bands, and many people with thee. Thus saith the Lord GOD; It shall also come to pass, that at the same time shall things come into thy mind, and thou shalt think an evil thought: And thou shalt say, I will go up to the land of unwalled villages; I will go to them that are at rest, that dwell safely, all of them dwelling without walls, and having neither bars nor gates, to take spoil, and to take a prey; to turn thine hand upon the desolate places that are now inhabited, and upon the people that are gathered out of the nations, which have gotten cattle and goods, that dwell in the midst of the land . . . And thou shalt come from thy place out of the north parts, thou, and many people with thee, all of them riding upon horses, a great company, and a mighty army: And thou shalt come up against my people of Israel, as a cloud to cover the land; it shall be in the latter days, and I will bring thee against my land, that the heathen may know me, when I shall be sanctified in thee, O Gog, before their eyes . . . And it shall come to pass at the same time when Gog shall come against the land of Israel, saith the Lord GOD, that my fury shall come up in my face. For in my jealousy and in the fire of my wrath have I spoken, Surely in that day there shall be a great shaking in the land of Israel; So that the fishes of the sea, and the fowls of the heaven, and the beasts of the field, and all creeping things that creep upon the earth, and all the men that are upon the face of the earth, shall shake at my presence, and the mountains shall be thrown down, and the steep places shall fall, and every wall shall fall to the ground . . . "* -- (Ezekiel 38:1-20)

Who or what is,"Gog . . . prince of Meshech and Tubal" (translated *prince of Rosh* in other versions)? It is without a doubt, modern Russia.

*Smith's Bible Dictionary* (Spire Books, page 584) says, "The meaning is, that Magog is the head of the three great Scythian tribes, of which "rosh" is thus the first.

"By Rosh is apparently meant the tribe on the north of Taurus, so called from the neighborhood to the Rha, or Volga, and thus in this name and tribe we have the first trace of the RUSS or RUSSIAN nation."

*Unger's Bible Handbook* (Moody Press) adds, "Some . . . identify it with Russia . . . the general area was that now occupied by Russia." In reference to the passage, *Lange's Commentary on the Holy Scriptures* (Zondervan) says, "Gesenius (the historian) observes that it can scarcely be doubtful that the first trace of the Russians is here given." C.I. Scofield DD, in *The New Scofield Reference Bible*, Page 881 (Oxford University Press) says, "The reference is to the powers in the north of Europe, headed by Russia." While *Thru The Bible With J. Vernon McGee* (Thomas Nelson Inc.) states, "Bishop Lowther made the statement that Rosh taken as a proper name in Ezekiel signified the inhabitants of Scythia from which the modern Russians derive their name."

The internationally respected Bible teacher, J. Vernon McGee looked to three evidences that, "The Prince of Rosh" is Russia. His first piece of evidence is what he called, "Linguistic Phenomenon." He not only quoted Bishop Lowther, but pointed to the fact that Russia was first called Muscovy, derived from Meshach. His second point is the fact of "Geographic Phenomenon." He said, "Now the second proof that identifies Russia is the geographic position. Here we have mentioned the nations which will be the Russia in the last days: "Gomer, and all his bands: the house of Togarmah of the north quarters, and all his bands: and many people with thee". "Gomer" is Germany, and "the house of Togarmah" is Turkey. "Of the north quarters" gives us the geographic location.

"Again in verse 15 we read: "And thou shalt come from thy place out of the north parts," and in chapter 39:2 the same location is given, " . . . and will cause thee to come up from the north parts." Whenever I give an illustrated message on the passage in Scripture, I always show a map of Israel and Russia. The literal meaning here is the "uttermost parts of the north." If you look at a map, you will find that Russia is directly north and northeast. Directions in the Bible are in relation to the land of Israel. North in the Bible does not mean north of California or north of where you live. In the Bible north is north of Israel, and south is south of the land of Israel. West is west of the land of Israel, and east is east of the land of Israel. In other words, Israel is the geographical center of the earth as far as the Word of God is concerned.

"Finally we come to the philosophical or ideological phenomenon, which helps us identify Gog and Magog with Russia. "And say, 'Thus saith the Lord GOD; Behold, I am against thee, O Gog, the chief prince of Meshech and Tubal.'" (Ezekiel 38:3). This is strange language. Here in the Book of Ezekiel, God has said several times that He is against certain nations. He said it about Babylon; He said it about Egypt; and He said it about the nations which were against His people and against His person. Now here is a nation that is to arise in the last days, a nation which is against God. The reason we know it is against God is because God says, "I'm against you." This makes it different from any other nation, because God has said this about nations already in existence that have exhibited enmity and rejection of Him, but this nation hadn't even come into existence when Ezekiel gave this prophecy. Yet God says he is against it."

We will look at the reason why God speaks so forcefully against Russia in the next chapter.

The above map of the "Ancient World" (published in 1901) shows the countries named in scripture -- Tubal, Gomer, Magog, Meshech, Cush, Phut (Put) and Togarmah.

# Chapter 4
# WHY THE MIDDLE EAST?

Why would Russia want to become involved in the Middle East conflict? To understand this, one has to become familiar with the Communist mind. To do this, we will look briefly at how that mind works.

Communism has a comprehensive and tight grip over a large number of people. In fact its influence is over an estimated 1.8 billion people -- 36% of the world population, over 1/3 of the world's surface. This hasn't happened over night. It has been a steadfast and progressive plan. Since 1917, 70,000 people a day have been forced to live under

Marxist/Leninist rule. Over 100 million people have been systematically and ruthlessly killed.

Every Communist has been taught a basic philosophy called "Scientific Dialectical Materialism." Those who don't know what SDM is and how it works, know next to nothing about the Communist mind. The authors of this belief were Carl Marx and Nicholai Lenin. It is a method of logic which is based on contradictory opposites. SDM is taught in every school of Communism in the world. All actions are derived from these perspectives. To understand the meaning of this, imagine someone who wants to leave a crowded room. His objective is the door; but to get to it, he may have to avoid groups of people in his way by digressing to the left or to the right. He doesn't head for the door, pushing and bumping into the groups in his path.

If you were watching him, not knowing his objective, when he turned from his pathway to the door, you may mistakenly think his purpose was another direction entirely. But his goal is always one of reaching the door, even though his direction may seem to suggest something else.

Or take for example the way a man drives a nail in with a hammer. When he hits the nail, he doesn't keep pushing down on it with the hammer, but draws it back to gain more power. To someone who has never seen how the process works, the person may seem to be doing the very opposite of his objective. It may look as though he has actually given up on hitting his goal of driving in the nail. But he who understands, knows that the withdrawal of the hammer, is as essential as the actual strike. Every Communist leader understands this simple philosophy of advance and retreat for the sake of the objective.

We can see Communism at work, with its continual advance through aggression and then retreat through peace talks. Take the time to think back on how many countries have been terrorized and raped by Communism, then think of the peace talks which have followed as some sort of appeasement for the Western world. A typical example was seen on January 30th, 1991, when the Soviets pledged to join with the U.S. "to promote Arab-Israeli peace," once the war in the Persian Gulf ended. At the same time, they gave assurances that they would pull back some of their troops from the Baltic republics of Lithuania, Latvia and Estonia, which they had invaded and pillaged in 1940. They failed to specify the number of troops, nor the timing of the withdrawal. With one hand they play policeman, with the other hand they play criminal. Estonia's Foreign Minister, Lennart Meri said, "Estonians watched the rape and murder during the annexation of Kuwait by Iraq in 1990, and paralleled it with what happened to their own nation when the Soviets invaded."

Russian leaders seem to bring hope to this war-torn world with sincere discourse, then fighting suddenly breaks out on a new front. The ideal, is to provide a leader who has charisma, one who would become so popular, one that U.S. so appreciates, it would have him as president. One who would take the Nobel Peace prize. Yet, the Gorbachev who spoke of peace, is the same Gorbachev who controlled the fighting in Afghanistan, supplied terrorists in Africa, and shipped arms to Nicaragua. Soviet leaders come to power because they are strict adherents to Marxism. They rise to the top because they are dedicated to the ideals of Communism.

Every past Soviet leader has committed violent aggression, followed by talks of peace -- Stalin, Khrushchev, Brezhnev and Gorbachev; advance through hostility, retreat through peace negotiations, then detente (a word which means a relaxing of tension).

To understand this principle further, think on how a sailboat advances. It will change its direction to take advantage of a certain breeze. Think of the advances the Soviets made when the U.S. was distracted by the Gulf Crisis. When there are winds of social unrest in a country, Marxism will exploit that issue for the purpose of advancement. They will develop it into a major social cause. It doesn't matter if they don't believe in the issue itself, what matters is whether or not it will be of long term benefit to Socialism. They will flow with the peace movement, civil rights, environmental issues etc. if they will further the goal. Even though they are totally committed to atheism, (Lenin said, *"Every thought of God is utter vileness"*) they will tolerate religion in order to gain influence within the religious community. They will even promote private ownership of land (as happened in Russia in 1990) to rally the support of peasants, then reverse their stand once in power (as happened in Russia in 1991). This philosophy explains why Communists can participate in peace movements on one side of the world, while waging war on the other. This is seen as justifiable in the Marxist mind, when it is in truth, nothing but wholesale hypocrisy. It also creates the illusion that there are different Communist movements, unrelated one to the other, but the committed Communist sees himself as merely one worker bee in the hive of Marxism-Leninism, whose aim is world-wide dominance of

Communism, and defeat of capitalism. He is happy just to be a part of that long range objective even though he knows that he may not live to see the end goal. The movement has no concern for the individual or for individual happiness. The entity is simply a tool of the state; he has no dignity or worth in himself.

Marxism and evolution are cozy bedfellows. The atheistic belief is that man has no spirit, he is merely an advanced animal, and therefore has no authority to answer to. Any thought of God is nothing but paganism . . . capitalist nonsense. Those who profess a belief in God are expelled from the movement, unless done dialically, for the purpose of advancement. The Bible and Marxism are utterly opposed to each other. The Scriptures contain the absolutes of Divine Law -- You shall not kill, You shall not steal etc., but Communism says, "The end justifies the means." It is a law unto itself. It sets itself above the Law of God, saying you may kill, steal and lie, for the goal. In fact, as I have said before, over 100,000,000 people have been systematically and ruthlessly murdered for the godless cause of Communism.

With so much innocent blood dripping from its lewd fingertips, it is easy to see why God is against the "prince of Rosh."

Joseph Stalin once manifest the true spirit behind Marxism when he said, "We have deposed the Czars of the earth, *and we shall now dethrone the Lord of Heaven!"* As time passed, Stalin became acutely paranoid of being assassinated, and each night he would lock himself in one of eight different bedrooms, letting no-one know which one.

His daughter, who was in the room at the time of his death, described what happened, "My father died a difficult and terrible death. God grants an easy death only to the just. At what seemed the very last moment, he opened his eyes and cast a glance over everyone in the room. It was a terrible glance, insane . . . and full of fear of death. Then he lifted his left hand as though he were pointing to something above, bringing a curse down on us all! The gesture was full of malice. *The next moment, the spirit wrenched itself free of the flesh."* Stalin dethroned.

# Chapter 5
# BETRAYED BY THE NAZIS

Lenin always understood the truth that a small band of committed men could control the masses. The Russian people overthrew the Czarist Government in 1917. Soon after, Lenin and his small band of revolutionaries subverted that elected democratic government. In 1920 the Communists consolidated control over Georgia, Armenia, Azerbaydzhan, the Ukraine, Byelorussia and Koshac; then in 1922 the Far East Republic and Turkestan. In 1924, they took the Mongolian People's Republic. All of these countries, each with its own culture and language were brought under the hammer and sickle and called the "Soviet Union." Once again, millions resisted, and millions died.

In 1939, the Soviets formed a pact with Adolf Hitler, joined with Germany and invaded Poland. They divided the country with the Nazis and then, the Russian Communists ruthlessly slaughtered and buried in mass graves over 10,000 Polish troops and officers in 1940. Then the Russian forces invaded Estonia and Lithuania, *in spite of their non-aggression pacts with Russia.*

In what military experts throughout the world declare to be one of the most incredible blunders in military history, Hitler abandoned his planned invasion of a vulnerable Great Britain and suddenly attacked Russia. The Soviets then declared themselves to be against Germany, pleaded for help against Nazi invasion, and were promptly rewarded with billions of dollars in American aid; (the U.S. did the same thing in 1990, when Russia petitioned her for help for her starving peasants).

At the end of the Second World War, Russia immediately took control of East Germany. When no complaints were heard, the Red Army quickly took over the rest of Eastern Europe. By the end of World War 2, the Communists established solid control over the Eastern European countries of

Albania, Bulgaria and Yugoslavia in 1946, Rumania in 1947, Czechoslovakia in 1948, Hungary and East Germany in 1949. Between 1949 and 1961 nearly 3 million Eastern Europeans fled the Communist dictators in their homelands through Germany into West Berlin. In 1956 in Hungary, Russian troops in armed tanks were sent in to crush the rebellion. There was a revolt led by students which succeeded in overthrowing the Communist puppet government. The young freedom fighters quickly broadcast radio messages to the free world asking for help. Their pleas fell on deaf ears. Three days later, the pitifully armed and helpless rebels were mercilessly crushed by the Soviet military. In 1968, Czechoslovakia revolted; it too was crushed.

When the brutal suppression of these uprisings raised strong protests in the West, the Marxists took a dialectic step backwards. They increased peace talks and cultural exchange activities with the West. The Marxist-Leninists gained momentum after World War 2, when North Korea fell under Communist rule; a Soviet trained Marxist was installed as a puppet dictator. At the same time, Mao Tse Tung (while receiving military aid from Mongolia), put into motion Communist takeover of China. Tibet was invaded in 1951. The Communists conducted a ruthless campaign of torture, rape and murder. Thousands of children were then abducted and taken to Red China for Marxist-Leninist indoctrination. Next to go under, was North Vietnam. South Vietnam fell to Communism in 1975. When Cambodia went under the hammer, 40% of its people were crushed by its ruthless hand. In the early 1960's Tanzania fell under its disguised control; then fell Algeria, Ethiopia, The Congo, Angola *and seven other African countries.*

Libya is a recognized extension of Marxist-

Leninist influence. Its dictator seized power with the help of Russia, Germany and Syria. Libya serves as a base of Marxist-Leninist aggression in North Africa. It has, by military force, invaded Niger and Chad. As Communist-trained troops in Chad provide a base of infiltration into the Sudan, so Ethiopia uses its border to impact the Sudan also. The tragic and much published famine in Ethiopia of the 1980's came as a direct result of Communist policy in that land.

In the Spring of 1978, Communist-trained Afghan officers seized the Afghanistan Presidential Palace. Even before the Afghan people were completely aware of the coup, the Marxist military turned the Government over to the civilian Afghan Communist party. Resistance to the puppet Government led to the 1979 invasion of 120,000 armed Soviet troops, who were supported by tanks and fighter planes. *Over a million Afghans were slaughtered.*

So with this basic understanding of the Soviet's insatiable lust for world dominance, it is easy to see why they should have interest in the Middle East. Yet this is more than likely only one of the reasons this region is so attractive to them, something we will look at in the next chapter.

# Chapter 6
# ARMAGEDDON OUTTA HERE!

The Bible even gives the Russian reasoning for and direction of the attack on Israel. Russia is ready; *The Reader's Digest* says, "The Soviets are entrenched all around the rim of the Middle East heartland -- In Afghanistan, South Yemen, Ethiopia, and Libya" ("Countdown in the Middle East", May 1982).

"Russia is continuing to maximize military strength . . . 55% of Soviet industry is still involved in military production" (*Firing Line,* William Buckley, January 1991).

It would seem from Scripture that nuclear weapons will be used in this battle, speaking of search parties looking for bones of those killed in the war. When the bone is located, it will not be touched, but "a marker" will be set by it; and it will be buried by special teams (Ezekiel 39:14-15), a more than possible reference to radio-active contamination. The Book of Joel (800 B.C.) also

speaks of this war, confirming the nuclear weapon aspect with "pillars of smoke" being seen during the battle (Joel 2:30). It seems that it even speaks of flame-throwing tank warfare. Not having access to the word "tank," the prophet describes his vision of these war machines with, "A fire devours before them . . . they climb the wall . . . every one marches in formation . . . they run to and fro in the city . . . they run on the wall . . . the earth quakes before them" (Joel 2:3-10). By December, 1988, the Soviet Union had in its arsenal 41,000 tanks.

One can only surmise as to the reasoning within the Soviet mind as to why it should attack the tiny nation of Israel, but it only stands to reason that it should be attracted to the incredible oil reserves in the Persian Gulf. Iran, in 1991 had oil reserves of 92.9 billion barrels, while Iraq had 100 billion barrels.

During the early days of the Middle East Crisis in which Russia was said to be keeping a low profile, *USA TODAY* reported, "The Soviet Union may be playing both sides in the gulf war, at once publicly supporting the allies yet positioning itself to preserve postwar ties to long-time client Iraq . . . Several times U.S. officials have been obliged to knock down reports that Soviets are providing Iraq with covert technical aid or intelligence. The Soviet military would be eager to help Iraq, if for no other reason than to salvage its prestige," says Jay Kosminsky, a defense policy specialist at the Heritage Foundation. "They built, trained and designed the Iraq military," Kosminsky says. To be "defeated overnight by the U.S." would be humiliating, he says."

*The Wall Street Journal* (February 4, 1991) said, "Efforts by the Soviets to expand their influence in the Middle East since World War 2 have mainly been disruptive of Western peace efforts. Gamal Abdel Nasser, the Arab strong man of the 1960s, was equipped by the Soviets and encouraged to conduct his ill-fated effort to crush Israel in 1967. The Palestine refugee camps -- those squalid breeding grounds for racial hatred -- have remained in place thanks in part to Soviet influence in the U.N.

"PLO and Gadhafi terrorists have received Soviet training and weapons. Iraq became a regional superpower thanks in large part to weapons and support from the Soviets. Syrian and PLO depredations in Lebanon have been conducted under the influence of Soviet military and KGB operations."

The Soviet Union supplied arms and military advisers to Iraq during its 8 year war with Iran (according to *National Geographic Society*, January 1991), and just prior to the U.N. resolution to oust Iraq from Kuwait, there were still over 2,000 Soviet military advisers in Iraq (*L.A. Times*). Both of those Arab nations have a deep-rooted hatred of Israel. *In fact, nothing would delight the Arab nations more, than to see Israel annihilated.* They hate the Jews with a vengeance. Hai Amin al Husseini (Mufti of Jerusalem) said in 1948, "I declare a holy war, my Moslem brothers! Murder the Jews! Murder them all!" In 1966, the then defence minister of Syria, Hafez Assad said, "We shall never call for nor accept peace. We shall only accept war. We have resolved to drench this land with your (Israel's) blood, to oust you as aggressor, to throw you into the sea." In April of 1990, the "Butcher of Baghdad," Saddam Hussein added his bit with, "In the name of Allah, we shall cause fire to devour half of Israel." The next day, Yasser Arafat said, "We say to the brother and leader Saddam Hussein - - Go forward with God's blessing."

This hatred has festered over the years under Arab humiliation. Since 1948, a continual cry has come from the Arab world to destroy Israel. In fact, since that year, the Israelis have lived in constant threat of being liquidated by the surrounding Arab nations, which outnumber them nearly 50 to 1. In

June of 1967, Israel was confronted with an Arab army which consisted of 653,000 men, 2,700 tanks, 1090 war planes and over two hundred ships. Israel's answer was 300,000 men, 800 tanks and a mere 19 ships. Despite the odds, to the Arab indignity, the Jews are still there. God said that no-one would remove them from their homeland. This was so evident during the six day war of 1967, when Israel took back old Jerusalem -- Israel suffered the loss of less than one thousand fatalities *in contrast to the death of thirty-five thousand Arabs.*

For the massive reward of oil, for the rich mineral deposits in the Dead Sea, the warm-water access ports of Israel, and for the advancement of the Communist cause, Russia may see fit to combine with the Arab nations to rid the Middle East of the "infidel" Jews. If that were the case, add to the Soviet arsenal of 41,000 tanks, the tanks of Iran, plus their hundreds of thousands of troops to the multitude of the forces of Libya, Ethiopia, Germany, Turkey and Russia, and you have the potential Armageddon. *The Wall Street Journal* (February 4, 1991) gives insight to the might of the Soviet military, " . . . with five million men under arms and their great array of warplanes, warships, missiles, nuclear warheads, tanks, rocket launchers and chemical and biological weapons, they are indeed a military superpower."

Israel will never have lasting peace until she obeys God. If she will obey His statutes and keep His Commandments, He will give her rain in due

season, an abundance of food, freedom from fear, victory over the enemy, and peace within the land (Leviticus 26:1-13). At present, Israel is relatively godless; in fact, Israel's ex-Prime Minister said in a recent T.V. interview that 70% of the nation is secular. Even during the Iraqi bombing of Israel, sales of pornographic videos, alcohol consumption etc. dipped only for a short time. Sadly, from what we see of Scripture, Israel will seek God only as a last resort, when she sees that she cannot prevail against the might and power of the Russian invasion (Joel 2:12-20). Deuteronomy 4:30 gives warning that it would take tribulation to turn Israel to God in the "latter days." When Israel finally turns to God in true repentance, God will take pity on His people and remove far from them the "northern army" (Joel 2:20).

Another sign of the "latter days" will be a clear understanding of the judgments and the will of God. No other generation has seen Russia mustering forces against Israel, the Arab-Israeli conflict in the Middle East, and the re-establishment of the Jews in Jerusalem. We can see the signs of the times all around us. The Jews are pouring out of Russia as God draws His people back to their homeland. *World Press* reports, "The fear that the state cannot protect its citizens has helped bring about an explosion in Jewish emigration. More than 18,000 a month have been leaving, compared with 914 for all of 1986. Many would-be-emigrants gather outside the Moscow synagogue on Saturday mornings." It is predicted that "most of the 200,000 or so Jews in Moscow and the 2 million throughout the country will leave . . . *Israel expects 1 million Soviet immigrants by 1992.* " (italics added)

No other generation has had the scientific knowledge to help it understand "strange" scriptures, nor have they had access to the Bible as we have, so that we can understand perfectly the times in which we live. "The anger of the Lord will not turn back until He has executed and performed the thoughts of His heart. In the latter days you will understand this perfectly" (Jeremiah 23:20).

As the attention of the world is focused on the tiny nation of Israel, and as you look at the strained faces of world leaders because of Middle East "complexities," remember Holy Scripture. God is very specific in His warning that, 1/ Jerusalem would be an insurmountable problem to the nations of the world and, 2/ That *no-one* would remove His people from their homeland -- "And it shall happen in that day that I will make Jerusalem a very heavy stone for all peoples; all who would heave it away will surely be cut in pieces, though all nations of the earth are gathered against it" (Zechariah 12:3).

The first time Jesus Christ came to this earth was as a "lamb," to die for the sins of the world. The

Second Coming will reveal Him as Judge of the earth.

Even though we live in fearful times, this is an extremely exciting hour for those who trust in the Savior, because it shows how close their redemption is -- when we will be transformed from these bodies of death into "immortal" bodies, with no more aging, pain, suffering and death. God will then take His curse off the earth and restore it under His perfect will with no more disease, famines, tornadoes, earthquakes, floods, droughts etc. Remember, the prophecies of scripture prove it to be the Word of God; it is *all* "God-breathed" and will surely come to pass (see 2 Timothy 3:16).

Look at this immutable promise from the Word of God:

*"Behold, I tell you a mystery: We shall not all sleep, but we shall be changed -- in a moment, in the twinkling of an eye, at the last trumpet. For the trumpet shall sound, and the dead will be raised incorruptible, and we shall be changed . . . So when this corruptible has put on incorruption, and this mortal has put on immortality, then shall be brought to pass the saying that is written: Death is swallowed up in victory"* (1 Corinthians 15:51-54).

Keep one eye on the Middle East and the other towards the heavens.

# Chapter 7
# EGO BLOW

It's been said that the worst thing you can ever say to another human being is, *"You are wrong!"* It is a sad indictment on the human race that the statement is probably true.

Even if the person is totally in the wrong, and you tell him so without discretion, you will more than likely alienate yourself from him with such a blow to his ego.

You may have picked up this book totally convinced that you were right in your beliefs. But as you read its pages, you began to see that there is another point of view; that the Bible is indeed the Word of God.

It is my hope that this revelation has come to you in a spirit of gentleness on my part, so that you won't feel alienated from me, because I want to speak from my heart to yours.

When I became a Christian, I found myself in a dilemma. The Bible told me, "There is none good, no not one." Yet I knew many good people. The problem was that God's definition of good and mine were different. We may say a man is "good," because he's stopped stealing and reformed his ways. We think that good is merely "not bad." God's definition of good is perfection . . . *in thought, word and deed.*

Millions are being "good," thinking that they will merit entrance into Heaven. In essence, they are trying to purchase everlasting life by offering their good deeds to God in exchange for it. On Judgment Day, it will not be seen as a mere offer for purchase, but a detestable attempt to bribe God to forget their crimes against His Law.

Do you know of anyone who's "good?" Was Mother Teresa good? No, she needed Jesus Christ as her Savior; she admitted her sins. How about Mahatma Ghandi? Was he good? No, he said, "It is a constant torture to me that I am still so far removed from Him whom I know to be my very life and being. I know it is my own wretchedness and wickedness that keeps me from Him." He acknowledged his sins. Perhaps the only good person you can find is yourself. In truth, what we are really doing when we say that there are plenty of good people, is attempting to justify our own sins. Let me speak to the wife of any man who says he's perfect. She will tell me the truth.

I once saw a T.V. news reporter say, "Tonight we will look at the buying and selling of the world's most priceless commodity. . . *information*." He was right, information *is* the world's most priceless commodity. If you have information as to where oil deposits are, or you have information about the location of gold or diamonds in the earth, you can be a billionaire overnight. *Information can even save your life*. If you are in a building that is on fire and you know the location of the fire exits, you can find your way out. If you are without that information, you will probably die. Your actions will be governed by information, or more precisely, what you *do* with that information will govern your actions.

A man in the U.S. once wanted to paint his steep A frame roof. As his ladder was too short to reach the top, he threw a strong rope over the roof, went around the other side, and carefully secured the rope to the back of his car. Then he went around the back of the house, climbed up onto his roof, tied the rope firmly around his waist, and began painting. His wife, not knowing what he had done, came out of the house, car keys in hand, got into the car *and drove off*. He was pulled over the top of the roof and was seriously injured.

Perhaps you see nothing wrong with having your own beliefs, even if they can't be substantiated. But remember, *your information will govern your actions*. If you believe a drink contains poison, you won't drink it. If you believe it is O.K., you will drink it. If you believe the theory of evolution is true, and from that premise believe that the Bible is false, you won't obey its precepts. Like the man who secured himself to the car, you will find you are only as secure as to that to which you secured yourself. If your faith is in evolution and not God's promises, you will find that what you have tied yourself to, will be your eternal downfall. You will perish because you refused information that would have saved your most prized possession.

## DIAMONDS OR WATER?

Let me put it another way. If I offered you a fistful of diamonds or a bucket of cool water, which would you take? The diamonds of course. But if you were crawling through a desert, lips blistered, tongue swollen, dying of thirst, and I offered you a fistful of diamonds or a bucket of cool water, you would despise the diamonds and whimper, *"Give me water. . .lest I die!"* That is called "circumstantial priorities." Your priorities change according to your circumstances.

Christianity demands a choice between the sparkling diamonds of sin and the cool, clear waters of everlasting life. Of course, we *far* prefer the diamonds of sin, something quite normal for sin-loving humanity. But on Judgment Day our circumstances will radically change. We will find ourselves in the desert of God's judgment, upon our face, about to perish under the burning heat of a Creator who warns us that He's a "consuming fire." We despised the Water of Life when it was offered to us in Christ. Now we must face eternal consequences. Those sparkling diamonds we so dearly hold will suddenly be the glaring evidence for our condemnation.

Imagine you and I are seated next to each other in a plane. I have very reliable information that the plane is about to crash. In fact, the whole aircraft is rocking and shaking to a point where it seems it may fall to pieces any moment. Still, I'm not too fearful, because I've reached under my seat, found a parachute and put it on. What concerns me is the fact that you don't see your need to put yours on! Even though you know you have to jump, you have three lines of argument as to why you should leave the parachute off. Firstly, you're adamant that the plane had no maker. Secondly, you have noticed that a number of the other passengers say they're wearing a parachute, when it's obvious to you that they are not. And thirdly, you haven't put it on because you think you can somehow defy the law of gravity.

I feel a bit embarrassed at having to point out to you that if the plane was made, there must be a maker. But after a while you see my reasoning. You also accept my answer to your second objection -- that if the other passengers wanted to pretend they were wearing a 'chute, they would find out their mistake when they jumped. My suggestion to you was, best get yours on first, then see if you can persuade "pretenders."

The third objection was also answered by simple logic. I found that the most effective way to convince you of your need, was to hang you out the door of the plane by your ankles. I feel at peace about having you put the parachute on for a motive of self preservation.

## THE MAIN OBJECTIONS
Let's now swing from this allegory to real life. We will say that your two main objections as to why you shouldn't accept the Savior were,

1/ Perhaps you didn't if know there was a God, or if the Bible was the Word of our Creator. Now because of prophecy etc. you are convinced.

2/ Hypocrisy in the Church. The Bible says God will judge hypocrites; when they die, they will see their error. You now understand that every person will give an account of *themselves*, not of each other.

Your problem now, is that you still somehow think that you don't *need* a savior -- someone to stand on your behalf, an advocate for your defence before the Judge of the Universe. You think you can somehow defy the Law of God. *Please,* trust me for a moment, while I attempt to "hang you out the plane door by your ankles." It will be a fearful experience, but it is necessary. It should have the effect of helping you to see the seriousness of what I am trying to say.

My aim is not to convince you of the existence of a moral Law, you already know it exists. The Bible says that the "work of the law" is written on your heart, that God has given "light to every man." You have always known that it is wrong to steal, to lie, etc. -- conscience has always been there as a judge in the courtroom of your mind, giving you knowledge of what is right and wrong since the time you can remember. No, my aim is to persuade you of the *consequences* of breaking that Law. To do this, all I require is for me to get a hold on the "ankles" of your honesty.

What we will do, is thoroughly go through the Ten Commandments to see if you have broken any of them. As we do so, remember these three facts:

1/ God sees the sins of your youth, as though it were yesterday. Just as time doesn't forgive transgression of civil law (i.e. a murderer is still a murderer twenty years after the crime), so time doesn't forgive sin.

2/ God sees your thought-life. He made the mind of man, so surely He can see what he made -- nothing is hid from His omniscient eye.

3/ He is perfect, just, good, holy and utterly righteous. By that, I mean, by His very nature, He *must* punish transgression. If He sees a murder take place, He must eventually bring the murderer to justice, something that the most dense of us can understand, even if there is disagreement on the *form* of punishment.

## THE LAW

It is important to realize that being a Christian doesn't determine that you will live eternally; it just defines the *location*. If you die, as Jesus said, "in your sins," God will judge you accordingly. There is no place in Scripture for "purgatory," for a second chance.

The Bible reveals that you and I have failed to put God first, to love Him with heart, mind, soul and strength. It states plainly, "There is none that seeks after God; there is none that understands." The First Commandment is to put God first in our affections. That's not an option, it's a command.

Imagine buying a child a toy for his pleasure, and having him love the toy more than he loved you. Yet isn't that what you've done with God? Didn't He shower the gift of life upon you; giving you freedom, food, family, eyes, ears, a mind to think with? And you used that mind to resist the very One who gave you the mind in the first place! Isn't it true that you have been guilty of complete and utter ingratitude? If someone gave you a car as a gift, should you thank them? Have you ever humbly thanked Him for the gift of life? If you have, but you've never obeyed His command to repent, then your "thanks" is nothing but empty hypocrisy.

If you love anything more than you love God, whether it is husband, wife, brother, sister, boyfriend, girlfriend, car, sport, or even your own life, you are loving the gift more than the Giver. What have you got that you didn't receive?

Everything you have came to you via the goodness of God. Jesus said that we should so love God that all our other affections for mother, father, brother, and sister, should seem as "hate," compared to the love we have for the God who gave them to us. It has been so rightly said, that if the greatest commandment is to love God will all our heart, mind, soul and strength, then the greatest sin, is failure to do so.

But more than that. The Bible says that the First Commandment also involves loving your neighbor as yourself. In the story Jesus gave of the Good Samaritan, the man picked up a beaten stranger, bathed his wounds, carried him to an inn, gave money for his care and said to the inn keeper that if he spent any more money while he was gone, he would pay his expenses. That is a picture of how God *commands* we should treat our fellow human beings. We should love them as much as we love ourselves . . . whether they be friend or foe. In fact Jesus didn't call that story the "good" Samaritan; he wasn't good, he merely carried out the basic requirements of the Law. Have you loved humanity as yourself? You be the judge; have you kept the Law? Will you be innocent or guilty on Judgment Day? I'm not judging you -- I'm asking you to judge yourself. Sentence for transgression of the First Commandment is death.

# Chapter 8
# HANG ON TIGHT

In the last chapter, you kindly allowed me to take hold of the ankles of your understanding, for the purpose of showing you your need of God's forgiveness. Now hold on tight as we go through the rest of the Law:

The Second Commandment is, "You shall not make yourself a graven image" (you won't find this in the Roman Catholic Bible; it was taken out because it exposed idolatry within the church. What they did was to break the Tenth Commandment up into two, to make up for the one they deleted). This command means that we shouldn't make a god in our own image, either with our hands or with our minds. I was guilty of this. I made a god to suit myself. My god didn't mind lust, a fib here or there; in fact he didn't have *any* moral dictates. But in truth, my god didn't exist. He was a figment of my imagination, shaped to conform to my sins. Almost all non-Christians have an idolatrous understanding of the nature of God.

Let me show you what I mean. Although the Bible says that humanity hates God without cause, most would deny that they do. You may not hate *your* god, but look at the Biblical revelation of our Creator: God killed a man in Genesis 38 because He didn't like his sexual activities. He commanded Joshua to kill every Canaanite man, woman and child, without mercy. He drowned the whole human race, but for eight people in the Noahic flood. He killed a man because he touched the Ark of the Covenant. He killed a husband and wife in the New Testament, because they told one lie! Now *that* God, says humanity, is not so easy to snuggle up against.

Before you ask why God killed a couple for telling a lie, ask, "Why didn't God kill me, when I lied for the first time!" All God did was to treat them according to their sins. When we did wrong for the first time and didn't get struck by lightning, we then concluded that God didn't see or didn't care about what we did, and with that, became more bold in our sin. Yet, all that happened was that God extended His mercy toward you and I, that we might have a time of grace to repent.

If we caught a revelation of what God is really like, we would fall flat on our faces in terror. Just take an objective look at some of His natural laws. If you break electrical or gravitational laws, the consequences are fearful, but they are merely a weak shadow of the eternal moral Law of God. My words cannot express what God is like, but His Law gives us some insight into His holy nature. The Law reveals utter holiness, supreme righteousness, and absolute truth. God has a violent passion for justice.

What has your understanding of God been like? Do you tremble at the very thought of His power and holiness? Have you seen Him in the light of Holy Scripture, or have you made up a god to suit yourself? If that is the case, you are guilty of idolatry. The Law's sentence for idolatry is death, and according to Scripture, no idolater will enter the Kingdom of Heaven.

The Third Commandment is, "You shall not take the name of the Lord your God in vain. For the Lord will not hold him guiltless who takes His name in vain." When a man hits his thumb with a hammer, he may express his disgust by using a four-letter filth word beginning with "s," or he may spit out the name *"Jesus Christ!"* The question comes to mind as to why he should use the name of a person in that situation. It does seem to make some sense that he used an unclean word like sh-t to express disgust, but why use the name of Jesus Christ? Why didn't he say, "Buddha!" or "Muhammad!"

What's so special about the name of Jesus? To answer that question, we have to go to the only source of information on the subject, the Bible. In it we see that God has, "highly exalted Him (Jesus) and given Him a name that is above every name."

According to the Bible, there is no other name on this earth that deserves honor and respect, than that of the name of Jesus Christ. When our profane friend used it in the way he did, he was substituting it for the word sh-t. *In other words, he aligns the Name with human excrement.* He counts them as the same thing. The Bible calls this "blasphemy," warning "the Lord will not hold him guiltless who takes His name in vain." In fact Jesus said, "The world hates me, because I testify of its deeds, that they are evil."

What greater verbal expression of hatred can

there be for someone, than to use their very name in such a context. Humanity doesn't even use the name of Hitler to curse. His name is not despised with the venomous hatred needed to qualify it for such use.

## JUST A WORD

Most who use God's name in blasphemy would deny that they are using it in the way I have described. In fact, when they blaspheme, they will often say that they don't even know that they are doing it. To them it's "just a word." If that is your justification, *then your own mouth condemns you.* You so count the name of God as nothing, it passes by your lips without even registering in your mind -- *you truly use it "in vain." Don't you realize what you are doing?* You are cursing the name of the very One who gave you life! Penalty under the Law for blasphemy is death.

The Fourth Commandment tells us, "Remember the Sabbath day, to keep it holy." I ignored this command for 22 years of my non-Christian life. Not for a second did I say, "God gave me life, *what does He therefore require of me?"* let alone set aside one day in seven to worship Him in spirit and in truth. Death is the sentence under the Law for Sabbath-breaking.

The Fifth is, "Honor Your Father and Mother." That means we are commanded to value them implicitly in a way that is pleasing in the sight of God. Have you *always* honored your parents in a way that's pleasing in God's sight? Have you always had a perfect attitude in all things towards them? Ask God to remind you of some of the sins of your youth. You may have forgotten them, God hasn't.

What is your most valuable possession? Isn't it your life? Your car, your eyes, your money, etc. are all useless if you are dead. So obviously your life is the most precious thing you have. If you are in your right mind, you will want to live a happy life, and live a long one; yet you have God's promise that if you don't honor your parents, you will have neither (Ephesians 6:1).

The Sixth is, "You shall not kill." But Jesus warned that if we get angry without cause, we are in danger of judgment. If we hate our brother, God calls us a murderer. We can violate the spirit of the Law by attitude and intent.

Maybe you have the blood of abortion on your hands. Civil law may smile upon your crime -- God's Law calls you a murderer and the Sixth Commandment demands your death.

The Seventh is, "You shall not commit

adultery." Who of us can say we are pure, when Jesus said that we violate this command in spirit, by lusting after a member of the opposite sex. He warned, "You have heard it said by them of old, "You shall not commit adultery," but I say to you, whoever looks upon a woman to lust after her, has committed adultery already with her in his heart." Until you find peace with God, you will be like a man who steals a T.V. set. He enjoys the programs, but deep within his heart is the knowledge that at any moment there could be a knock on the door, and the law could bring him to justice.

Remember that God has seen every sin you've ever committed. He has seen the deepest thoughts and desires of your heart. Nothing is hid from His pure eyes. The day will come when you have to face that Law you have broken. The Scriptures say that the impure (those who are not pure in heart), the immoral (fornicators -- those who have sex before marriage) and adulterers will not enter the Kingdom of God. Adultery carries the death penalty.

The Eighth is, "You shall not steal." Have you ever taken something that belonged to someone else? Then you are a thief. You cannot enter God's Kingdom. You may have stolen a book from a library, failed to pay a parking fine, or maybe you "borrowed" something and never returned it.

God is not impressed with the *value* of what you stole. When you have stolen, you have sinned against your God, you have violated His Law.

The Ninth Commandment is, "You shall not bear false witness." Have you ever told a fib, a "white" lie, a half truth, and exaggeration? Then you have lied. How many lies do you have to tell to be a liar? Just one -- *"All* liars will have their part in the Lake of Fire" (Scripture cannot be broken). You and I might not think that deceitfulness is a serious sin. God does.

The final nail in our coffin is, "You shall not covet." That means that we should not desire things that belong to others. Who of us can say we are innocent? All of us has sinned. As the Scriptures say, "There is none righteous, no, not one; There is none that understands, there is none that seeks after God." Just as with civil law, you don't have to break ten laws to be a law breaker, so the Bible warns, "Whosoever shall keep the whole Law, yet offend in one point, the same is guilty of all." The most blind of us will usually admit that man has glaring faults, because we are forever transgressing against each other. But our transgressions are vertical, not horizontal; our real crimes are against God, not man.

# Chapter 9
# DON'T CLEAN UP YOUR LIFE

Without the Law, we look at sin from the standard of man; we have a distorted view. It takes the Law to give us insight to His standard, which is utter perfection. The Bible asks, "Who shall ascend the Hill of the Lord? -- He that has clean hands and a pure heart;" "Blessed are the pure in heart, for they shall see God;" "Be perfect as your Father in Heaven is perfect." How do you measure up? Are you perfect, pure, holy, just and good? Or have you caught a glimpse of what you must look like to God? The picture the Scriptures paint of us is not a nice one.

This may sound strange, but the worst thing you can do at this point of time is to say that you will change your lifestyle. You will, from this day forward, live a good life. Let's say you were actually able to do that; from now on you will always not only *live* a good life, but *think* pure thoughts. Who then is going to forgive your past sins! Can a judge let a murderer go free because he promises to live a good life from now on? No, he's in debt to justice. He must be punished.

The truth is, you have violated the Law a multitude of times. The Law, like a dam of eternal justice, has been cracked in numerous places and is towering over your head waiting to burst upon you. The Bible says, "the wrath of God" abides on you. Jesus warned that if the stone of a just and holy God falls on you, it will "grind you to powder." When you grind something to powder, you do a thorough job. Every foul skeleton in the closet of every human heart, will be brought out on the Day of Judgment. Nostradamus was right when he said, "From the sky will come the great King of Terror." The Scriptures warn, " . . . when the Lord Jesus shall be revealed from Heaven with His mighty angels, in flaming fire taking vengeance on them that know not God, and obey not the Gospel of our Lord Jesus Christ: who shall be punished with everlasting destruction from the presence of the Lord, and from the glory of His power" (2 Thess. 7-10).

The thought may have entered your mind that perhaps God will overlook your sins. Perhaps He, in His mercy, could just look the other way. If He does so, then He is unjust. Think of it again in connection with civil law. Can a judge look the other way when a criminal is obviously guilty, and be true to what is right? Even if the judge feels sorry for the criminal, he must stay true to the law, justice must be done. In the ten years between 1980 and 1990, in the United States alone, there were 60,000 murderers *who were never caught!* At least 60,000 murders were committed, and the murderers got away totally free. No doubt the figure is higher as many "accidents" and "suicides" are actually murders in disguise. These are people who have raped, tortured and strangled helpless victims; cutting up their bodies, or burning them without trace. Should God overlook their crimes on Judgment Day? Should He turn a blind eye? Should He compromise eternal justice? Or are you saying God should punish only the *serious* crimes? But your lying, stealing, adultery of the heart and rebellion *are* serious in His sight. No, the Bible says He will by no means clear the guilty. Who would like to see justice overlooked? Isn't it only the guilty?

Well, what is the punishment for sin? The Bible warns of everlasting damnation. It speaks of eternal Hell. Imagine if Hell was just a place of continual thirst. Have you ever had a thirst where you thought you'd die for lack of liquid? Or imagine if it were only a place of gnawing hunger? Or merely chronic toothache? Have you ever been in pain where you feel you want to die? Have you ever felt the pain of a broken arm, leg or rib? The Scriptures warn that Hell will be a place of "weeping and gnashing of teeth;" a place of eternal torment; a place where death will not bring welcome relief to suffering. A place where God will withdraw every blessing He has showered upon sinful, rebellious, ungrateful humanity. An abode where there will be absence of color, goodness, peace, beauty, love and laughter. A place of darkness, depression and despair, where murderers, rapists, those who have tortured, those who have stolen, lied, hated, been greedy, lustful, envious, jealous, blasphemous and rebellious to the command of God will dwell. Hell is the place where sinful humanity will receive its just retribution for crimes against the Law of a Holy God. *How terrible sin must be in the sight of God, to merit such just punishment!*

How's your conscience? Is it doing its duty? Is it accusing you of sin? Is it affirming the Commandments to be right? If not, which of the Commandments do you say is unjust -- "You shall not steal," "You shall not bear false witness," "You shall not kill"? Perhaps you have committed adultery, or you have been longing for opportunity to. While no human being can point a accusing finger at you, the Ten Fingers of God's Holy Law stand as your accuser. You have been caught holding a smoking gun. The Law calls for your blood. Under it, the penalty for adultery is death by stoning. I don't stand as your accuser, I hang my head in guilt as one who has been in your place. I, like every other red-blooded male, was an adulterer at heart. I could not, in good conscience, call for justice to take its course.

## CAUGHT IN THE ACT

You are like the woman in the Bible, caught in the very act of adultery. The Ten Great Rocks of the Law are waiting to beat down upon you. My earnest prayer is that you will not attempt to justify yourself at all, but bow your head and agree with the Law and the impartial voice of your conscience, and say, "Guilty! . . . what must I do?"

In doing so, you are merely saying that God's

testimony about humanity is true; that our hearts *are* deceitfully wicked, to a point of not only being vile sinners, but of being so deceitful that we will not even admit our own sins!

Like the woman, you have no other avenue to take. Your only hope is to fall at the feet of the Son of God. Ironically, there is only One human being who can call for justice to be done. And yet He is the only one who can forgive sins. At His feet alone, is the Law satisfied. If you humbly call on His name, you will hear, "Where are your accusers?" and be able to say, like the woman, "None Lord."

How could this be? Did God somehow compromise His justice through His Son. No! His justice was *satisfied* through His Son. What has happened is that the Law has stirred up the judge of conscience. The reason you could sin and not be concerned, was because the judge had been wooed into a deep slumber. The thunderings of the Law awoke him and now he stands as your accuser. There is an air of indignation that he has been silenced for so long. He has come back from his slumber with a vengeance, and with each Commandment he says, "Guilty!" What then must you do to satisfy his charges? No monetary payment will quieten his accusation of liability; no prison sentence will silence his righteous charge. What is it that will free you from the torments of what the world calls a "guilty conscience"? The Bible says that there is only one thing that can do it -- the blood of Jesus Christ, " . . . How much more shall the blood of Christ, who through the eternal Spirit offered Himself without spot to God, *purge your conscience from dead works* to serve the Living God?" (italics added). In other words, anything you might try to do to save yourself from the consequences of sin, is nothing but "dead works."

Let's go back to civil law. Imagine you had broken the law. You are guilty of some terrible crime. You don't have two beans to rub together; *there's nothing you can do to redeem yourself.* Justice is about to take its course, when someone you don't even know steps into the courtroom and pays the fine for you! If that happened, the demands of the law are totally satisfied by the one who paid your fine. You are free to go from the courtroom. *That's what God did for you and I.* When the Law utterly condemned us, Jesus Christ stepped into the courtroom and paid the fine for us by His own precious blood.

Words fail me to express His love which was demonstrated to us on that cross so long ago. When the Law called for our blood, Jesus gave His. When the justice of a holy God cried out for retribution, Jesus cried out on the cross in agony as He satisfied it, by giving Himself on our behalf. The Law didn't just demand the death of the Son of God, it demanded the *suffering death of the perfect, sinless Messiah.* Sin is such a serious thing in the sight of God, the only thing that would satisfy His righteousness was the unspeakable suffering of a sinless sacrifice.

Let's go back to the plane analogy for a moment. Imagine if I had spent a great deal of effort in trying to persuade you to put your parachute on, by talking to you about the horrible consequences of breaking the law of gravity. I had been "hanging you out the plane by your ankles," speaking of what would happen to you if you hit the ground at 120 mph.

Your eyes widened as I went into details. But, slowly it dawned on you that if you wanted to live, you had better put the parachute on. Suddenly, you are convinced. It needs no more words from me.

With trembling hand, you reach under your seat, *to find to your horror that there is no parachute!* Terror *really* gets a grip on you now, as you think of the horrific death you have to face at any moment.

As you sit there in a daze, you are awakened

from your living nightmare by a kindly voice. Another passenger you have never seen before, is holding a parachute out for you to take. You reach out and take it in your trembling hands. Words can't express your gratitude. An unspeakable joy fills your heart, as you realize that you don't have to die. The thought as to where the stranger got the parachute from hardly enters your mind.

After the jump, you find that every one of the other passengers have lived . . . *all but one*. It's only then you realize that the stranger gave you his own parachute, *and went to his death so that you could live*.

That is what Jesus Christ did for you. He gave His life that you might be saved. A complete Stranger, Someone you didn't even know, did that for you. His was a willing, terrible, substitutionary death.

## WHAT SHOULD YOU THEN DO?

What you must do, is for the first time in your life, truly obey the command of God to repent and put your trust totally and singularly in Jesus Christ. Your alternative is to have the full fury of God's Law unleashed against you on Judgment Day. You have no other option -- *unless you repent, you shall perish*. There is no purgatory, no second chance, no other name, no other hope, no other way for you to be saved. Pray a prayer like this from your heart:

"Dear God, I have violated your Law. I have broken your Commandments. I have sinned against You and You only. You have seen every thought and deed. You saw the sins of my youth, and the unclean desires of my heart. I am truly sorry.

I now understand how serious my transgressions have been. If justice was to be done, and all my sins uncovered on the Day of Judgment, I know I would be guilty, and justly end up in Hell. Words cannot express my gratitude for the substitutionary death of the Lord Jesus Christ. I may not have a tear in my eye, but there is one in my heart. I *really* am sorry.

From this day forward, I will show my gratitude for your mercy by living a life that is pleasing in your sight. I will read your Word daily and obey what I read. In Jesus' name I pray, Amen."

# Chapter 10
# PLAYBOY CHRISTIAN

America is undoubtedly the most Christian nation on earth. It has an incredible 1,485 Christian radio stations broadcasting the Good News throughout the land. But more -- there are over 300 Christian television programs also beaming out the Gospel, not only across this nation, but to the farthest corners of the earth.

Christianity is part of her culture . . . a tornado hits Texas; a woman thanks the Lord on secular television, for what she considers to be a miracle in being preserved from the twister. A quiz show host asks contestants for an example of a "life-changing experience." Without hesitation someone answers, " . . . Accepting Jesus Christ as Lord and Savior." Gospel music is ever popular, with music festivals being sponsored by big business's such as McDonalds. *Time* carries a comprehensive interview with evangelist Dr. Billy Graham; the President reads his Bible daily; supermarkets and drug stores carry Christian plaques with the Lord's Prayer and the Ten Commandments on them. Bibles and other Christian books also adorn their shelves. There are more "fish" on cars than there are in the supermarkets.

According to *The Church Today,* the Barna Research Group gathered statistics revealing that 62% of Americans say that "they have made a commitment to Jesus Christ that is still important in their life today." So accordingly, the United States of America then has a staggering 148 *million* professing Christians! In fact *T.V. Guide* reported that an amazing 96% of Americans believe in God. The foundation of America is soaked in a godly heritage. The Pilgrim father's *reason* for establishing the country was, "for the glory of God and the founding of the Christian faith." Its Declaration of Independence states that "all men are endowed by God with certain inalienable rights." Fifty of the fifty-five men who instituted its

Constitution were professing Christians. What other nation has "In God we trust" on its currency and a national anthem proclaiming that God's grace was shed upon it? If ever a nation should shine with God's blessing, it is this nation.

The Bible says that righteousness exalts a nation, that its health will "spring forth because of righteousness." God will honor any country that honors Him, with the blessings of long life, health and prosperity. If America is as godly as its seems, it will be reflected in her land. Instead, we are seeing the very opposite. In 1989 a flu virus killed 52,000, while 160,000 died of cancer. An estimated 2,500,000 people have Alzheimers disease, while in 1989 more people died of AIDS *than were killed in the entire Vietnam war*, not to mention the millions who have other sexually transmitted diseases. Despite a new wave of health consciousness, it is estimated that heart disease will, in time, claim 60,000,000 Americans. The country has gone from having one of the world's lowest infant mortality rates, to one of the highest, *with an incredible 40,000 babies dying each year*. More than 10,000,000 Americans suffer from asthma, 400,000 from Parkinson's disease, while The National Alliance for Mental Illness diagnose 10,000,000 as having serious, long-term mental illness. State institutions can house a mere 119,000, many of the rest roam the streets of big cities.

There are a million teenage runaways each year, thousands of suicides, escalating marriage breakdowns, wide-spread alcoholism, epidemic drug problems, boiling racism, and massive financial pressures from the home, to commerce. Add to that the fact that tornadoes, hurricanes, floods, earthquakes and droughts rock the nation, and it is hard to equate it all with God's blessing. The sad fact is, that this nation, which has a form of godliness, draws near to God with its lips, but its heart is far from Him. Contemporary America is merely being treated according to her sins -- Ezekiel 14:13 says, "Son of man, when a land sins against Me by persistent unfaithfulness, I will stretch out My hand against it . . . "

Despite her belief in God, in 1989 Americans spent $240,000,000,000 on gambling. Each year 5,000 women are killed by domestic violence, with a total of 23,000 murdered annually; while drunk drivers kill 25,000 people yearly. In 1989 120,000 women reported being raped. The number one killer of children are parents. In fact, also in 1989 2,500,000 abused, missing and abducted children were reported. The U.S. has *one hundred times* as many burglaries per capita as "godless" Japan. The list of 30,000 law officers already killed in the line of duty, is being added to almost daily. Grisly satanic murders and mass killings are commonplace. Drive-by shootings and other gang and drug related murders are beyond police control in many cities. Back in September 1987, *Time* recorded Florida State Representative Michael Friedman as saying, "The message we're sending out is, We can't protect you any more, so get yourself a gun and do the best you can." Violence, and drug usage has so infiltrated the pubic school system, that over 500,000 children have parents who have chosen to educate their kids at home.

Home video has taken porn and sexual violence into a new realm, while regular acts of violence spew out of T.V. programs at the rate of 38 every hour. Literally millions buy, and feed on pornography via socially accepted glossy magazines and adult-rated movies. In fact pornography has become a $32,000,000,000 industry. Few understand the truth that a nation sins and sicknesses go hand in hand. *USA Today* reported that recent movie censorship means that a wider audience can now feast on very explicit heterosexual and homosexual acts, stating that movies "can now start where most sex scenes end." Ironically, an article on the same page showed sharp increases in cancer, but *"researchers do not yet know why."* The answer is just across the page of the paper. The blessing of health is dependant on righteousness.

There are 50,000 drug-addicted children born each year in California alone, with 60,000 intravenous drug users in the city of San Francisco. In a desperate effort to halt widespread police corruption and drug usage, authorities in California resorted to lie detector tests for applicants, and found that 64% of those applying for the force were former drug users.

Jails are often so full, judges are dismissing cases because they have nowhere to put the criminals. The blood of the unborn is spilled at a rate of over 1,000,000 each year -- 146,000 of these abortions are done *when the mothers are in the 7-9 month stage of pregnancy.* The law deals out a year in prison for destroying an eagle's egg yet condones the murder of the unborn at 4,300 per day -- 97% for convenience. Millions of Americans have given themselves over to the perversion of homosexuality. Every year 800,000 babies are born to unwed teenagers.

## COSMETIC CHRISTIANITY

A 1990 survey in schools found that 40% of the kids had at least three sexual partners. They follow the adults example: *USA TODAY* disclosed that between 50-60% of married men had committed adultery, with the women not far behind. This however is not confined to the unchurched. A recent survey on university campuses uncovered that nearly 50% *of those who called themselves "evangelicals"* thought that premarital sex was O.K. In fact a confidential study done by *Christianity Today* among pastors, showed that *nearly one in four had been involved in some sort of sexual sin!*

Just before his death, Sammy Davis Jr publicly thanked Jesus for standing by him during a bout with throat cancer. When questioned if he had faith in Christ, he said that it was more cultural than a "religious thing."

I once spoke to a young man about Christian things. During the conversation, he not only spoke as though he'd been raised in a sewer, but right in the middle of his profanity he used the name of Jesus Christ in blasphemy. When I asked him if he had a Christian background, I was surprised to hear that he was not only a church-goer, but he considered himself to be a Christian. When I objected to the fact that he had just blasphemed, he said, "Everyone slips now and then." -- *Not that much.*

Contemporary Christianity is summed up by one

man I saw standing in a line. He was wearing a
cross and a Playboy bunny on the same chain.

# Chapter 11
# LOOK TO THE BASE OF THE TREE

**W**hat has happened? Why is there so much corruption inside, and outside of the Church? In this final chapter, we will look at the cause of the dilemma of the contemporary Church, and the sequential demise of the nation.

A recent survey in Great Britain found that approximately 50% of people asked about John Newton's song, "Amazing Grace," thought the hymn was about an *amazing* woman named "Grace." God's incredible grace (His unmerited favor) demonstrated in the cross of Jesus Christ, is indisputably the greatest truth the Church has to offer the world. "For God so loved the world that He gave His only begotten Son, that whoever believes in Him should not perish, but have everlasting life" is the very essence of our message. As a partaker in the mercy of God, it has always been my desire, (and no doubt it's yours if you know the Lord), as to how we may most effectively communicate God's love and grace to dying humanity.

This passion to reach the lost was somewhat frustrated some years ago, when I came across some alarming statistics which rang true, not only in my own experience and in the local church at which I was an associate pastor, but also among the many churches at which I had the privilege of ministering God's Word. The statistics concluded that as many as 80% and sometimes 90% of those who made commitments to Christ, from local church to large crusades, were slipping away from the faith (see our publication *Hell's Best Kept Secret*, Whitaker House).

In my search for the reason, I prayerfully studied the Book of Romans and found myself asking the question as to the purpose of the Law of God (the Ten Commandments). I was amazed at what I found. To answer this extremely relevant question, we will firstly look to the Scriptures, then to the godly counsel of Luther, Spurgeon, Wesley, Tyndale, Bunyan, Finney, and Matthew Henry.

My understanding had been that when the Bible spoke of the Law as being a "schoolmaster to bring us to Christ," it was referring to the Jew only, because the Gentile comes to the knowledge of salvation "by the hearing of faith." Yet Romans 3:20 tells us - "The Law was given to stop every mouth, and leave the whole world guilty before God." Its purpose was to stop *every* mouth, and to leave the *whole world* (not just Jews) guilty before God. The Scriptures do not make a division between Jew and Gentile when it comes to the ignorance of sin -- "There is *none* that understands, there is *none* that seeks after God (Romans 3:11 emphasis added). If the "work of the Law" was enough to give the knowledge of sin, why then did Paul see fit to use the essence of the First and Second of the Ten Commandments in Athens to preach against idolatry? It was because Paul knew they were ignorant (Acts 17:23,30) and that the Law would show them they had sinned against a holy God, for its intent is also to be God's instrument to bring "the knowledge of sin" (Romans 3:20).

Notice that this is confirmed by 1 Timothy 1:8, in that the Scriptures don't confine the lawful use of the Law to Jews only -- "Knowing this, that the Law is not made for a righteous man *but for the lawless and disobedient, for the ungodly and profane* etc." (italics added). It doesn't say "lawless and disobedient Jews, ungodly Jews, profane Jews" etc. In fact, in Romans 7:7 Paul said that he didn't know what sin was until the Law told him -- "Nay, I had not known sin, but by the Law." Was Paul more ignorant of sin than modern man? Was his conscience insufficient, while modern man's is? He knew sin from a human viewpoint, but the Law showed him sin in its true light, that sin "was exceeding sinful" (Romans 7:13), for without the Law, "the sense of (sin) is inactive" (Romans 7:8 Amplified Bible).

Is the Book of James for Jews only? Did James exclude the Gentiles when he spoke of becoming "convinced of the Law as transgressors" (James 2:9). If so, he should not have used the word "whosoever" in the following verse when he said, "For whosoever shall keep the whole Law, and yet offend in one point, he is guilty of all" (James 2:10). If the Law was only for the Jews, why didn't he then say, "For if a Jew shall keep the whole Law, yet offend in one point, he is guilty of all." No, James knew the Law was given to stop *every* mouth. The Jew, like the Gentile, is also saved by the "hearing of faith": -- "Wherefore the Law was our schoolmaster to bring us unto Christ, *that we might be justified by faith"* (Galatians 3:24 italics *added).* Both the Jew and the Gentile are saved by faith in Jesus Christ, apart from the Law.

Nowhere does Scripture say that the Law "saves." We are all saved by grace through faith. It is faith in the Gospel which is the "power of God to salvation." What the Scriptures do teach, is "The Law of the Lord is perfect, *converting* the soul (Psalm 19:7 italics added)." What then is the difference between *converting* the soul, and *saving* the soul? To illustrate the distinction, imagine you and I are in a plane which is about to crash. I had my parachute on, but you don't see your need to put yours on. The surest way for me to convince you of your need is to hang you out the plane by your ankles . . . just for a few seconds. Suddenly your knowledge of the consequences of breaking the law of gravity converts you from the way you were thinking, to the way I want you to think, to a point where you will not only accept the parachute, but also appreciate its function. Knowledge of the law of gravity changed your mind, but the parachute will save your life.

The function of the Law is not to save, but to convert the mind from a false sense of security, to seeing the utter danger of passing through the door of death without the Gospel. The Law changes the mind, but the Gospel saves the soul.

If the Church prefers not to mention the Law in Gospel presentation, which of the Ten Commandments do they find to be outdated and therefore superfluous for modern man? Which, would they say should not be applied to the sinner's conscience -- "You shall not kill . . . you shall not steal . . . you shall not commit adultery? Should we assume the average person has the knowledge of sin without the Law? Has he more knowledge than Paul and therefore doesn't need to be awakened by the Law? Why does he so vehemently break the Sixth Commandment and kill, declaring it a "right" to take the life of the unborn? Why does he break the eighth and steal, giving this country one hundred times more burglaries per capita as "godless" Japan? Why is the Seventh broken so carelessly? Adultery is so prevalent that nearly 60% of married men admit to the sin. The answer is evident -- the Church has failed in its responsibility to thunder the holy Law of God from the pulpit. Without the Law, the world will be a "law unto themselves," and perish through "lack of knowledge" of the Law (Hosea 4:6).

They will remain in self-righteousness, despite the "work of the Law, written in their hearts." They will go about to "establish their own righteousness, being ignorant of the righteousness which is of

God." They are ignorant because we haven't given them the Law of Sinai; to lift up our voice like a trumpet and show this people their transgression (for "sin is transgression of the Law" (1 John 3:4)). We have left sinners thinking that sin is horizontal rather than vertical; they are ignorant of the fact that they are sinning against God, and God alone in their transgression.

What greater example of using the Law in evangelism can we go to, than to the feet of the Master? Jesus, at the beginning of His ministry stated that He had come to preach the Gospel (not the Law) to the poor, the broken-hearted, the captives, the blind and the bruised (Luke 4:18). The Gospel of Salvation is for the poor in spirit, for those who mourn over their sinful condition, those who are bound and blinded by sin. Those who say they are rich and righteous and in need of nothing, will not accept grace. The Gospel is a "stumblingblock" to them. Scripture says God gives grace to the humble. The Gospel of Grace is only for the humble, for the proud will not receive it. It is for the Nathaniels and those who come in the humility of Nicodemus, for the devout, as those who gathered on the Day of Pentecost . . . those who had been humbled and brought to nothing by the Law. That's why Jesus gave both Nathaniel and

Nicodemus grace. That's why Peter made no mention of sin, Law, righteousness etc. at Pentecost, because each knew the Law and thus had a heart prepared for mercy. The Law made them "hunger and thirst for righteousness."

Read Luke 10:25 and see how Jesus used the Ten Commandments to bring the knowledge of sin to a proud professing expert of God's Law. See Him use seven of the Ten Commandments on a self-righteous sinner in Luke 18:18. See how the Law drove the adulterous woman to Christ in John 8, or how the Seventh Commandment steered the woman at the well to the Savior in John 4. Look at how Jesus used the law in Matthew 15 and Mark 7, specifically the 1st, the 3rd, 5th, 6th, 7th, 8th, 9th and 10th Commandments. Notice that Jesus actually quoted the specific Commandments (Mark 10:19, Matthew 5:28), so did Paul (Romans 2:21,22), so did James (James 2:11). Do the same. Do you want to be great in God's Kingdom? Jesus told us how we could be -- by being a teacher of the Law (Matthew 5:19). In doing so, you will drive sinners to Christ.

More than ever, the Psalmist's plea is relevant to the Church, "It is time for you to work O Lord for they have made void Your Law." The Church has negated the "key of knowledge" (Luke 11:52). It has laid aside the instrument God has given to convert the soul (Psalm 19:7). In contrast, Paul (the Apostle of grace) said he delighted in the Law (Romans 7:22). The Bible says it is "holy, perfect, just and good." In fact God promised that He would magnify the Law and make it honorable, while James calls the Ten Commandments, the "Royal Law" and the "perfect Law of liberty."

I was privileged to be involved in a move of God in the early seventies where one church received national publicity because in one short period it obtained approximately 800 decisions for Christ. There is no denying the fact that this was a genuine move of the Holy Spirit, and the fruit of that move can still be seen. Numbers of drug using, long-haired hippies were transformed by God and are now serving Him as successful pastors. However, of the 800 "saved," one would be fortunate to find 100 still going on in the faith. During that time, decisions were made solely through the "hearing of faith." The message was singularly the love, mercy and grace of God, no Law was preached.

How much better it would have been if the Law had been used to bring the knowledge of sin and we had seen the type of results which issued from the ministries of men like Spurgeon and Finney (who had an 80% retention rate in his converts). Instead, from this one church, we now have 700 sinners who have been inoculated to the Gospel by a method of preaching which cannot be substantiated by Scripture. In fact a method warned against by Spurgeon and Finney and so many others who were so mightily used of God.

True, lasting fruit can be seen from the "believe and repent" approach. There are those who enter a church building and remain within its walls by the hearing of faith without the Law, and after a time of hearing God's Word expounded, they then come to a place of repentance and are saved. But take your eyes off the top of the tree and look for a moment to the pile of rotten fruit at the base of the tree -- see not only the masses of inoculated and bitter backsliders, but see the multitude who never made it to the repentance stage, and sit within the Church with a false sense of assurance that they are saved. No matter how much they believe, they cannot be saved without repentance (Luke 13:3), and how can a man repent if he doesn't know what sin is? Paul said, "I had not known sin but by the Law."

Look at the harvest of the rotten fruit of sin in the Church, from pew to pulpit. The reason the Biblical order is "repent and believe" is so the sinner will leave his sin outside the Church doors.

A lawless Gospel will almost certainly produce lawless converts, those who name the name of Christ but never "depart from lawlessness," those who will hear those fearful words, "Depart from me you workers of lawlessness, I never knew you."

Let's now look to the counsel of the godly in this matter. Matthew Henry, perhaps the greatest Bible commentator of all time said, "As that which is straight discovers that which is crooked, as the looking-glass shows us our natural face with all its spots and deformities, *so there is no way of coming to that knowledge of sin which is necessary to repentance, and consequently to peace and pardon, but by comparing our hearts and lives with the Law.*" Matthew Henry maintained that there is no other way to come to the knowledge of sin and thus repentance other than by the Law of God. Who could maintain that a man can be saved without a knowledge of sin or repentance, and still remain faithful to scripture?

So what then happens when a man enters a church building and makes a decision by the "hearing of faith" without the Law? Charles Finney gives us the answer -- "Evermore the Law must prepare the way for the Gospel. To overlook this in instructing souls, is almost certain to result in false hope, the introduction of a false standard of

Christian experience, and to fill the Church will false converts. Time will make this plain." Finney says a lawless Gospel will have a three-fold effect, false hope, the introduction of a false standard of Christian experience and it will fill the Church will false converts.

Charles Spurgeon (the Prince of Preachers) was just as adamant. He said, "Lower the Law and you dim the light by which man perceives his guilt; this is a very serious loss to the sinner rather than a gain; for it lessens the likelihood of his conviction and conversion . . . I say you have deprived the Gospel of its ablest auxiliary (its most powerful weapon) when you have set aside the Law. You have taken away from it the schoolmaster that is to bring men to Christ . . . they will never accept grace till they tremble before a holy and just Law. Therefore the Law serves a most necessary and blessed purpose, and it must not be removed from its place." One hundred years later, it has been removed from its place.

John Wesley, in looking at ways a preacher may make "void the law through faith" said, " . . . the way for a preacher to make it all (the law) void at a stroke, is, not to preach it at all . . . when it is done with design; when it is made a rule, not to preach the Law; and the very phrase "a preacher of the Law" is used as a term of reproach, as though it meant little less than an enemy of the Gospel. All this proceeds from the deepest ignorance of the nature, properties, and use of the Law. The ordinary method of God is, to convict sinners by the Law, *and that only*."

Martin Luther in a sermon entitled "A Beautiful Sermon on the Law and the Gospel," published in 1537 said, " . . . we would not see nor realize it (what a distressing and horrible fall in which we lie), if it were not for the Law, and we would have to remain forever lost, if we were not again helped out of it through Christ. Therefore the Law and the Gospel are given to the end that we may learn to know both how guilty we are and to what we should again return."

Then Luther puts his finger on why this truth has been almost entirely extinguished from the Gospel presentation -- "This now is the Christian teaching and preaching, which, God be praised, we know and possess, and it is not necessary at present to develop it further, but only to offer the admonition that it be maintained in Christendom with all diligence. For satan has continually attacked it hard and strong from the beginning until the present, and gladly would he completely extinguish it and tread it under foot." Satan hates this teaching, because it is the key God has given to see this world reached with the Gospel of salvation. He will do anything to keep you from earnestly praying, "Open my eyes Lord, that I might behold wondrous things out of your Law."

John Bunyan (writer of *Pilgrim's Progress*) said, "The man who does not know the nature of the Law, *cannot* know the nature of sin." John Wycliffe, the Bible translator said, "The highest service to which man may attain on earth, is to preach the Law of God." Why? Because it will drive men to the Savior.

Notice that none of these godly men makes a difference between Jew and Gentile when it comes to the necessity of having the knowledge of sin, before they may repent and believe the Gospel.

Space doesn't permit me to quote further from Spurgeon, Wesley, Moody, Finney, Whitefield, A.B. Earl, John Newton, Augustine and other men God has used greatly to extend His Kingdom. Each, in his own way, is adamant that the Law must proceed the message of faith or the result will be false conversions, or as John Newton so aptly put it, that we might be preserved from "being tangled by errors on the right hand or on the left."

Perhaps you have had the unfortunate experience of hearing a harsh legalistic preacher and you equate that with being a "preacher of the Law," which has left you hesitant to expound the Commandments. Then look to Jesus as your example, and remember we are called to preach with compassion, with gentleness, and with tears. The Law will only condemn the guilty. The Commandment is a lamp and the Law is light . . . abandon it and you will leave the sinner in darkness as to his danger.

Maybe you don't want to offend sinners with the Law. Which then do you consider to be the greatest offense, to come under the thunder of God's Commandments and from there to flee from the wrath to come, or to spend eternity in unutterable agony in the fires of Hell? If the Law doesn't drive sinners to the Savior, it will drive them into the Lake of Fire (Romans 2:12). By forsaking the Law as the converting instrument of God, the Church is trifling with the souls of men. We must be utterly true to Scripture and to ourselves in our evangelical endeavors. If a doctor's aide waters down a prescribed medicine because he feels it will offend the patient, and the sufferer perishes, who is responsible for his death? Perhaps the greatest injustice we can do to a sinner, is to give a lawless gospel, then the assurance he is saved when he is not. This is what the modern Gospel presentation does.

If you really want to magnify the virtues of God's character, the beauty of His holiness, then preach His Law. If you want to show the depth of His love, of His grace, of His mercy, preach the Law. The only way to show mercy as mercy, is to display justice first. If you want to magnify grace, then open the Law, and from there show the sinner the extreme our God went to that He might redeem us from the curse of the Law, through the blood of His cross.

What else can I say, other than to plead with you to prayerfully consider these thoughts. I can think of no stronger way of ending this reasoning other than to say, if we continue making void the Law through faith, we will find we are working for the devil rather than for God. For every 1,000 decisions we get, as many as 900 will backslide, and of the 100 who remain in the local church, as many as 70 will be lukewarm in the areas of prayer, holiness, reading the Word and evangelizing the lost. Such "evangelism" is a furtherance to the work of satan and against the purposes of God, who desires that none perish but all come to repentance.

## WILL AMERICA FIGHT RUSSIA?

I heard once about a young man who didn't know the Lord. A husband and his wife were witnessing to him over a meal, when the husband said, with tears in his eyes, "If someone came through that door with a gun, and said he was going to shoot you or my wife, I would say to shoot my wife, because I know she would go to Heaven . . . *but you would go to Hell!*

The youth quickly looked across at the wife to see her reaction. With tears in her eyes, she nodded in agreement. The young man broke down at such love, and was soundly saved.

I wonder if you are as challenged as I was when I first heard that story. Do we love humanity enough to give up that which we cherish most, that they might be saved? May God give us that depth of compassion for the lost.

The sobering question which may be going through you mind as you think of the great conflict between Russia and Israel, is, *"Will the United States be drawn into the battle?"* Truly, God only knows; but I for one wouldn't be surprised to see the stars and stripes firmly planted next to Israel's standard. And know this, God will only stretch out His Holy Hand for America, if she obeys Him. In recent times we have heard our President call the nation to prayer. As much as this sounds pious, our nation doesn't lack prayer . . . *it lacks repentance.* Our President needs to name the shameful sins of

America -- the slaughter of the unborn, the rape of our women, the homosexuality, fornication, adultery, the violence of our entertainment, the greed, the corruption, the squalid literature that fills our stores. We need a voice that will lift up as a trumpet and show  this people their transgressions . . . that they have sinned against the Law of a holy God. They must be warned that if the absolute Justice of God isn't satisfied in Christ, it will find satisfaction in Hell, for Law without consequence is nothing but good advice. Then and only then will they flee to Jesus Christ and find the righteousness that appeases the wrath of a Holy Creator. Then and only then can we have confidence that God will deliver His own, for we are not His own  until we are born of His Spirit. At such a time, we may say with the Psalmist, "He that dwells in the secret place of the Most High shall remain stable and fixed under the shadow of the Almighty (Whose power no foe can withstand). I will say of the Lord, He is my refuge, my God, on Him I lean and rely, and in Him I (confidently) trust! For then He will deliver you from the snare of the fowler and from the deadly pestilence. (Then) He will cover you with His pinions, and under His wings shall you trust and find refuge; His truth and His faithfulness are a shield and buckler. (Then) You shall not be afraid of the terror of the night, nor of the arrow (the evil plots and slanders of the wicked) that flies by day, Nor of the pestilence that stalks in darkness, nor of the destruction and sudden death that surprise and lay waste at noonday. (Then) a thousand may fall at your side, and ten thousand at your right hand, but it shall not come near you." (Psalm 91:1-7 Ampl.)

On March 30, 1863, President Abraham Lincoln proclaimed, " . . . it is the duty of nations as well as men to own their dependence upon the over-ruling power of God; to confess their sins and transgressions in humble sorrow, yet with assured hope that genuine repentance will lead to mercy and pardon."

Only through the merits of Jesus Christ, can a nation become righteous in God's sight. Nations are made up of individuals, so may your *individual* repentance be perpetual. Keep yourself in the love of God; obey the Word to the letter, and let His Spirit impart life to you and to others. Seek to bring others to the knowledge of salvation. With the help of God we can do it.

God, in His great forbearance has helped us in past battles, such as in the recent Gulf Crisis. When He could have brought judgment, He extended mercy. Both political and military leaders were amazed at the comparative ease with which we were able to overcome Saddam Hussein's Middle East military might. When God could have humiliated the United States of America through defeat, He allowed victory. He condescended to answer the humble prayers of millions of Christians throughout the earth.

The might and deception of our eternal enemy is far greater than that of any natural military power. If we are to see victory in the battle for the souls of men in these closing hours of time, we must keep out hearts pure before our Creator, and take His exceedingly great and precious promises at face value, "For the eyes of the Lord run to and fro throughout the whole earth, to show Himself strong on behalf of those whose heart is blameless toward Him" (2 Chronicles 16:9). If God be for us, who can be against us!

"The enemy is in front of us . . . the enemy is behind us . . . the enemy is to the right and to the left of us -- *they can't get away this time!*"
                              -- General Douglas MacArthur

* * *

*Other publications by Ray Comfort include:*

*Hell's Best Kept Secret* -- $7.75
*God Doesn't Believe In Atheists* -- $7.75
*Someone Left The Cake Out In The Rain* -- $4.95
*In Search Of New Jawbones* -- $5.50
*Militant Evangelism* -- $4.95
*Springboards For Budding Preachers* -- $5.50
*You've Got To Be Choking!* -- $4.95

(California residents please add tax)

For a complete selection of books, booklets, tracts, and tapes by Ray Comfort, send a stamped, self-addressed envelope to:

Living Waters Publications
P.O. Box 1172
Bellflower
CA 90706

Over/

## ORDER FORM (*Russia will attack Israel*)

Bulk orders of this publication may be purchased at a special price of $1 per book -- **minimum order 25 copies.**

California residents please add tax.

Please send me ........ copies of *Russia Will Attack Israel*:

**NAME**.....................................................

**ADDRESS**
**(Print clearly)**.........................................

.........................................................

Send this form and your payment to:

**Living Waters Publications**
**P.O. Box 1172**
**Bellflower**
**CA 90706**